A

SAINSBURY COOKBOOK

—

THE COOKING OF
THAILAND

D1614751

INDONESIA AND
MALAYSIA

SRI OWEN

CONTENTS

Published exclusively for J Sainsbury plc
Stamford House Stamford Street
London SE1 9LL
by Martin Books
Simon & Schuster Consumer Group
Fitzwilliam House 32 Trumpington Street
Cambridge CB2 1QY

ISBN 0 85941 692 5

First published April 1991
Second impression October 1991

Printed in Italy by Printer Trento

THE AUTHOR

Sri Owen was born in central Sumatra, where her father founded a school and her grandmother managed the family rice-fields and coffee plantations, and cooked superb meals. When she was seven years old, the family moved to Java, her mother's home, and there she grew up and went to school and university. As a young university lecturer, she met her English husband and came with him to London in the mid 1960s. For many years she worked as a broadcaster and producer in the BBC Indonesian/Malay Service, and wrote her first book, *The Home Book of Indonesian Cookery,* published by Faber in 1976. This was followed by *Indonesian Food and Cookery* (Prospect Books, 1980/1986) and *Indonesian and Thai Cookery* (Piatkus, 1988).

Sri, her husband and younger son now live in Wimbledon, where she writes about food, cookery and restaurants, and gives cookery demonstrations. She is a member of the Guild of Food Writers.

KEY TO PHOTO ON PAGE 8:

1 *Thai basil;* **2** *fresh ginger;* **3** *light soy sauce;* **4** *raw peanuts;* **5** *shrimp paste;* **6** *bamboo shoots;* **7** *dried shiitake mushrooms;* **8** *fermented black beans;* **9** *dark soy sauce;* **10** *kaffir lime leaves;* **11** *yard-long beans;* **12** *fresh coriander;* **13** *fish sauce;* **14** *tamarind pulp;* **15** *baby corn;* **16** *dried shrimp;* **17** *candlenuts;* **18** *kaffir lime (whole);* **19** *tofu;* **20** *bean-thread noodles;* **21** *lemon grass;* **22** *small hot chillies;* **23** *large red chillies;* **24** *black glutinous rice;* **25** *yellow bean sauce;* **26** *fresh galingale;* **27** *bean sprouts;* **28** *water spinach;* **29** *white glutinous rice;* **30** *large green chillies.*

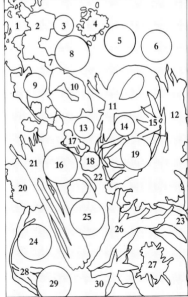

Satay Daging
(Beef satays, page 33)

Bubur Ketan Hitam
(Black rice porridge, page 90)

Babi Kecap (Pork in soy sauce with mushrooms,
page 55)

Pat Pak Ruam M
(Stir-fried mixed gree
vegetables, page 6

INTRODUCTION

*Pisang Goreng
(Fried bananas, page 91)*

Indonesia, Malaysia and Thailand are near
neighbours, but they are different in unexpected
ways. Malaysians and Indonesians are closely
related; Thais are distinct in race, language and
religion, though southern Thailand blends
into the peninsula of West Malaysia and
shares many traditions with it. All three
countries lie across traditional East–West
trade routes and have been deeply influenced
by India, China, the Arab world and Europe.
But they all have vigorous traditions of their
own, and keep what is best from the past while
they welcome what is new.

Of course all three lie entirely
within the tropics and share
more or less the same climate

*Sambal Goreng Udang
(Prawns in rich coconut-milk sauce,
page 39)*

*Acar Kuning
(Mixed cooked
vegetables in
piquant sauce,
page 71)*

*Nasi Goreng
(Fried rice, page 87)*

Note on quantities
*All recipes in this book give
ingredients in both metric
(g, ml, etc.) and Imperial
(oz, pints, etc.) measures.
Use either set of quantities,
but not both, in any one
recipe.*
    *All teaspoons and
tablespoons are level,
unless otherwise stated.
1 teaspoon = a 5 ml spoon;
1 tablespoon = a 15 ml
spoon.*
    *Egg size is medium (size
3), unless otherwise stated.*

of heat and high humidity. They all have hilly areas which are cooler and fresher, as well as long coastlines and coastal plains, with seas and rivers full of fish. They all grow a lot of rice, and on the whole they all have good fertile soil. They all produce a great quantity and variety of fruits, some long familiar in Europe, others just beginning to be known here. They share a taste for spices, having grown and traded them for centuries, as well as cooking with them, liberally but with subtlety and good judgment. In all three countries, chilli peppers – introduced from central America in the sixteenth century – have become practically a staple ingredient and condiment, though I must add that this food doesn't have to be chilli-hot. A touch of chilli is fine, but no more than is needed to bring out the flavours.

All over South-East Asia, food and hospitality are inseparably linked. Drink is of little or no importance, especially in Moslem areas where alcohol is discouraged. Sharing food is equally a duty and a pleasure; on the one hand, food must not be wasted or thrown away, on the other it must always be seen to be plentiful. This lavishness was unfortunately misunderstood by some Europeans during the colonial period, and a false tradition grew up, in Indonesia, of loading the *rijsttafel* or rice-table with a vast array of dishes and expecting everyone to eat far more than they wanted or was good for them. The real tradition, of family eating and of party food, was that all the dishes were set out on a kind of buffet, for people to take what they wanted, coming back for more whenever they wished. There was a variety of dishes so that everyone could find things they liked. The leftovers would reappear for the family breakfast, or in a big house would feed servants and poor relations in the kitchen.

The last twenty years have seen social change and economic development on a huge scale, and food habits have changed as well. Middle-class city-dwelling housewives, with full-time jobs but no longer with live-in help, use the new

Preparation and cooking times

Preparation and cooking times are included at the head of the recipes as a general guide; preparation times, especially, are approximate and timings are usually rounded to the nearest 5 minutes.

Preparation times include the time taken to prepare ingredients in the list, but not to make any 'basic' recipe, such as coconut milk.

The cooking times given at the heads of the recipes denote cooking periods when the dish can be left largely unattended, e.g. baking, stewing, and not the total amount of cooking for the recipe. Always read and follow the timings given for the steps of the recipe in the method.

kitchen technology of electric ovens and food processors. Their husbands, too, begin to take an interest and a pride in cooking. They give western-style dinner parties where the food is served in courses instead of all at once, and is expected to come to the table hot. But they use the ingredients and spices that they were brought up on and can buy cheaply in the neighbourhood market, and they adapt, as their predecessors did, the old dishes and techniques to the new opportunities.

This book will show you simple ways to prepare and serve real Indonesian, Malaysian, and Thai dishes at home. I am confident, from more than twenty years' experience of cooking for my family and friends, and from almost ten years of cooking professionally, that many of these dishes will become part of your regular repertoire and will be demanded over and over again by whoever sits at your table. This doesn't mean, though, that you have to cook a complete exotic menu every time. Remember the Asian genius for borrowing and adapting. Any of the dishes in this book, by itself, can form part of a meal which is otherwise familiarly English, French, Italian or whatever. You can start with pasta, go on to a Thai or Indonesian main course, and finish with apple pie; or serve some spicy starters before an English roast and tropical fruit as dessert.

People may tell you that spicy food will ruin the taste of your wine, and that only beer will be able to stand up to these strong flavours. I don't think this is completely true. A well-chilled sparkling or dry white wine, and a full-bodied fruity red wine, go with this food just as well as does a cold lager.

INGREDIENTS AND SPECIALITIES

CANDLENUTS
Indonesian, *kemiri*; Malaysian, *buah keras*. These are not unlike macadamia nuts. They are used in many recipes, always crushed or ground before being mixed with other ingredients. Raw macadamia nuts are a satisfactory substitute; in some cases blanched almonds can also be substituted, and I have suggested this where possible. Most Far-Eastern-food shops now stock candlenuts. Don't eat candlenuts raw – they are mildly toxic until cooked.

CHILLIES
Indonesian, *cabé*; Malaysian, *cabai*; Thai, *prik*. Although chillies are so important in South-East Asian cooking today, they were only introduced to this area in the sixteenth century, when seeds and plants were brought from Central America. There are of course several kinds of chilli. The two things to remember are: the smallest chillies are the hottest; and the hottest part of the chilli is the seeds. That's why many of these recipes tell you to take the seeds out. Chillies can irritate the skin, especially if you are not accustomed to handling them. Rub a little salt on your hands before you start cutting them up, and wash your hands afterwards. Keep your hands away from your face and eyes while working with chillies. If you do get the juice in your eye, it will smart uncomfortably; wash the area with plenty of cold water.

COCONUT
Indonesian/Malaysian, *kelapa*; Thai, *maprao*. Coconuts play a central role in the cooking of South-East Asia. Genuinely young ones, alas, are rarely available in Europe. The 'fresh' brown hairy ones you buy in the supermarket are fine, and for a few of these recipes I think it is worth the trouble of cracking one open and prising out the flesh. This always comes away with a brown skin on its surface. If the flesh is to be used for making coconut milk, this skin need not be cut away because its colour will not affect the finished dish. If, however, the flesh is to be used in a salad or a sweet, the skin should be discarded before grating.

COCONUT MILK
For most dishes, the 'coconut milk' that is specified (*santan* in Indonesian and Malaysian, *nam katee* in Thai) is not the liquid that you can drink from a newly-opened nut, but is the milk extracted from the flesh. It can easily be made from fresh grated coconut (that is how we make it in countries where coconuts and labour are plentiful), but in the west it is more conveniently made from desiccated coconut.

If you use fresh grated coconut, one nut will make about 600 ml (1 pint) of

A selection of Far-Eastern ingredients (see page 3 for details).

medium-thick milk. Pour hot water over the grated flesh and leave to stand until lukewarm. Then squeeze the flesh to extract the milk, and pass through a sieve to separate the liquid. The more water you use, the thinner the milk will be. The recipe may specify 'thick (or thin) coconut milk'. One nut will produce about 300 ml (½ pint) of thick milk. When cooking with coconut milk, never cover the pan.

COCONUT MILK FROM DESICCATED COCONUT
To make thick coconut milk, use 175 g (6 oz) of desiccated coconut and 600 ml (1 pint) of water, as described below. Then follow the same procedure again, using the same amount of water, to make a thin coconut milk. By mixing the two extractions you will get a medium–thick coconut milk, which is the standard thickness for most dishes.

If you have a blender, liquidiser or food processor, put in the desiccated coconut and pour on *half* the water, which should be hand-hot. Run the blender for 20–30 seconds, then strain the mush through a fine sieve, squeezing it as dry as you can. Put the coconut back into the blender, add more water and repeat the blending and sieving.

If you don't have a blender, put the desiccated coconut in a saucepan, pour the water over it, bring to the boil and simmer for 4–5 minutes. Allow to cool until hand-hot, then sieve and strain as above.

Coconut milk can be stored in the fridge for only 24 hours.

COCONUT CREAM
This is the thick white liquid that separates and gathers at the surface if you refrigerate coconut milk. A few recipes specify the cream, and you simply spoon it off as required. If you want the milk, however, just stir the 'cream' back into the clearer liquid beneath.

CREAMED COCONUT
The creamed coconut that you can buy in blocks is fine if the recipe asks for coconut milk to be added just before the dish is served, or for a very short cooking time, but it must be stirred all the time, otherwise it curdles. It is a convenient way of thickening a sauce that turns out at the last moment to be thinner than it should be. Cut off the amount you need from the block, then dilute it with a little hot water before adding it to your dish.

CANNED COCONUT MILK
This has recently become more easily available. It is very convenient, but for me much less satisfactory than the milk made from desiccated coconut. Shake the can well before opening it. Never keep unused milk in the can; transfer it to a glass bowl and keep in the fridge for no longer than 24 hours.

INSTANT POWDERED COCONUT MILK
This is obtainable in many ethnic shops; it is of course a little quicker and less messy than using desiccated, but results are much less good. I would use it only in emergencies.

CORIANDER LEAVES AND ROOTS

Indonesians use only the seeds, but in Thailand they use the leaves, stalks and roots as well. It is becoming easier to buy fresh coriander in England. Unfortunately the long roots are often cut off because it is assumed the plant 'looks better' without them; but in any trayful, a few will have a reasonable amount of root left on. Roots can be frozen – leave a short piece of stem on each root before wrapping for the freezer.

FERMENTED YELLOW OR BLACK BEANS

Indonesian/Malaysian *tauco*; Thai, *tow jeow*. These are used in dishes of Chinese origin, and are easy to find, in tins or in jars, in Chinese, Malaysian or Thai shops. For the black fermented beans, the dried ones in small boxes or plastic bags are better than the tinned ones in brine.

FISH SAUCE

Thai, *nam pla*. This is a salty, savoury, appetite-whetting sauce which is used in many Thai dishes and has much the same function as soy sauce – *kecap* – in Indonesian /Malaysian cooking.

FLAT-LEAF PARSLEY

This is also known in the UK as 'continental' parsley.

GALINGALE OR GALANGAL

Indonesian, *laos*; Malaysian, *lengkuas*; Thai, *ka*. This is a rhizome or root, rather like ginger but with a somewhat mellower taste. Fresh galingale, which is available in ethnic shops, can be chopped like ginger. The Thais use more of it than their neighbours do, especially in soup, such as Kai Tom Ka (page 20). It is also available dried. If using a large piece of dried galingale, remember to take it out before serving. Laos or galingale powder is also available.

GINGER

Many of these recipes specify fresh ginger, and I suggest that it should be either chopped or sliced finely, or put into the blender with other ingredients for the paste. If you don't like ginger or can't buy fresh ginger, use a little powdered ginger instead. It will make its own small contribution to the overall effect. Pickled ginger is also available in jars; it is very good and can be used instead of fresh ginger.

GROUNDNUT OIL

This is also known as peanut oil, and is easily available in the UK.

KAFFIR LIME

Indonesian, *jeruk purut*; Malaysian, *limau purut*; Thai, *makrut*. A type of citrus fruit found in many parts of South-East Asia; now available in Thai shops in London and elsewhere. The leaves (*daun* in Indonesian and Malaysian; *bai* in Thailand) are also used a great deal, and the Thais use the rind (*piw makrut*) as well. In some recipes, bay leaves can be substituted, and I have suggested this where possible.

LEMON GRASS

Indonesian, *sereh*; Malaysian, *serai*; Thai, *takrai*. This herb, which does look like a coarse, heavy type of grass, is used in many recipes for its mildly sour-sweet, citrus flavour. It can be bought, fresh or ground, in many Asian shops and some supermarkets; or it may sometimes be persuaded to grow as a house plant. It is sold in stems about 15 cm (6 inches) long, with the tough but fragrant outer leaves trimmed short. For most dishes, cut the stem into 3 equal lengths; one of these pieces is usually sufficient. Remember to remove it before serving. For Thai curries, soups and salad dressing, the outer leaves are stripped off (they can still be used in cooking, as above); only the tender heart is used, chopped into rounds like a spring onion and added to other spices to be blended into a curry paste. For soups and salad dressing you just use these tiny thin slices raw.

NOODLES
There are of course many types, just as there are of pasta. Here are the most common ones.

Egg noodles: these look very like spaghetti, except they are usually sold in tangled yellow blocks, not bunches of straight sticks. You can occasionally buy fresh ones in Chinese shops, but the dried ones in packets are really just as good and will keep for months. There are round ones and flat ones.

Rice vermicelli: these are very thin, and sold in what looks like a skein of whitish wire. A thicker type are rice noodles and are labelled 'rice sticks' – these are like bundles of narrow white ribbon.

Bean threads: also called cellophane noodles, because they are colourless and almost transparent. These are also very thin. They are made from mung beans.

PALM SUGAR
Indonesian/Malaysian, *gula merah*; Thai, *nam tan peep*; Anglo-Burmese, *jaggery*. This is made from the juice of the coconut-palm flower; it is dark red-brown in colour, and hard. To use it,

grate the block, or break a piece off and dissolve as directed.

PANDANUS
Packets of these long narrow leaves are now fairly easy to buy, fresh. They are also called screwpine leaves. They are used for colouring and flavouring.

PEANUTS
Indonesian and Malaysian, *kacang*. Use raw, unsalted peanuts, which are easy enough to obtain in most areas. They are used in South-East Asia because they are cheap, filling and nutritious. To make Sambal Kacang (A peanut sauce, page 76), do not peel off the reddish inner skins, as these will give a good colour to your sauce and taste better as well.

RAW PRAWNS
Some of these recipes call for raw prawns, which are the kind that would usually be bought in the Far East. They can be difficult to come by here however, so if you can't find fresh or frozen raw prawns you can substitute cooked

ones. Cooked prawns will usually need a minute or so less cooking time than specified in the recipes.

RICE

As an Indonesian, I have to say that the best rice available in the west for the purposes of Indonesian, Malaysian and Thai cookery is 'Thai fragrant' rice – there are several brands on sale. Although it may be described as 'perfumed' on the bag, the only fragrance is a pleasant smell of freshly-cooked rice that issues from the kitchen at dinner time. I always cook my rice in an electric steamer, using 1–1¼ cups of water to every cup of dry rice; this gives the rather moist, slightly sticky boiled rice that Indonesians like. If you prefer harder, separate grains, you can use a little less water or go for basmati or some other type.

Glutinous or 'sticky' rice is used mainly for making sweets, but it is also eaten as a staple main-course food and is well worth trying. It is more filling than ordinary long-grain, so don't cook quite as much as you normally would. Most short-grain rice is rather sweet and one variety is used mainly (by the British anyway) for rice pudding. There is nothing wrong with processed or boil-in-the-bag or instant rice, except that it is more expensive and, to my mind, a bit bland.

Black glutinous rice is also used for making sweets. I have included one particularly delicious example, Bubur Ketan Hitam (Black rice porridge, page 90).

SAMBAL

This is the Indonesian and Malaysian word for a hot chilli relish, which is used both in cooking and as a condiment. You can make your own, or buy it from most Asian food stores and many supermarkets. 'Basic' sambal is simply crushed red chillies and salt, and is called *sambal ulek* (often spelled *oelek*). But there is a whole repertoire of sambals to which other highly-flavoured ingredients have been added, e.g. *sambal manis* (sweet and relatively mild), *sambal kemiri* (with candlenuts), *sambal udang* (with prawns), etc.

SHIITAKE MUSHROOMS

Dried shiitake are available in most Oriental stores. They need to be reconstituted by soaking in hot water for 30 minutes or more, when they become soft and easy to slice. Fresh shiitake are available in large supermarkets. They can be sliced very thinly or just quartered, and need very little cooking. The stalks, especially when dried, are hard; use them in the stock pot, to enhance the stock with a delicious extra flavour.

SHRIMPS, DRIED

These small dried shrimps are not hard to get, provided you have a Chinese, Malaysian or Thai store within reach, but they are surprisingly expensive. They are usually roasted before being packaged. Soak in cold water for 10 minutes before use, then chop or put in the blender or crush with pestle and mortar.

SHRIMP PASTE
Indonesian, *terasi* (also spelled *trassie*); Malaysian, *balacan* or *blacan*. This is an extremely pungent, salty, hard paste which is used throughout Indonesia, Malaysia and Thailand, but only in very small amounts. If in doubt, use less rather than more. It is sold in blocks, and I usually slice the block or cut it up and put the pieces in an airtight jar for storage; it keeps almost indefinitely. For many recipes, the paste is grilled or fried before use. It can then be crumbled so that you can measure it with a teaspoon.

The Thai version, *kapi*, is usually sold in a plastic tub, and is softer, so it can be spooned out from the tub. 'Raw' paste is crushed or blended along with other spices for dishes in which the spiced paste is then fried.

SOY SAUCE
(OR SOYA SAUCE)
Indonesian and Malaysian, *kecap* (and therefore pronounced 'ketchup' – it is the same word); this dark-coloured, salty-tasting liquid has been produced from soya beans, by a complicated process of fermentation, for centuries. The familiar commercial brands are perfectly good for any of the dishes in this book. Some recipes, however, specify light or dark soy, and there is a perceptible difference in taste. By and large, light soy sauce is thinner and saltier, dark is thicker and sweeter. All soy sauces are strong-tasting and must be used sparingly; even the darkest contains a lot of salt.

TAMARIND,
TAMARIND WATER
This is important for giving to dishes the faint sourness that counteracts and gives depth to the sweetness of much South-East Asian food. Many of my recipes specify tamarind water, which is made by simmering a chunk of dried tamarind pulp in water for several minutes, letting it cool and then squeezing and pressing it to extract the juices and flavour. Discard the remains of the pulp and put the dark, unappetising liquid in with the rest of the ingredients. It will taste good. If you use tamarind water often, it is worth making a small stock of it; it will keep in the fridge for at least a month. Put a whole 500 g (1 lb) block into 1.5 litres (2 pints) of water and simmer till the liquid has reduced by half. Let it cool, then squeeze and sieve as before, boil for 10 minutes to purify it further, and store it in an airtight jar.

TAMARIND SLICES
These can now be bought in many Chinese shops. Strictly speaking, they are not tamarind, but they achieve exactly the same effect. You do not need to boil or squeeze them – just put a couple of slices in the pot while cooking. Remember to take them out before serving.

TOFU
Indonesian and Malaysian, *tahu*; Thai, *tow hoo*; better known in the west by its Japanese name, *tofu* or

14

beancurd. It can be obtained in most supermarkets and good oriental food stores, either fresh or fried. Fresh tofu has a short life; kept cool, and submerged in water, it will last for three or four days. Fried tofu must also stay cool (but not in water); it will last about a week. 'Everlasting' or 'silken' Japanese tofu will keep unopened for a year or more, even without refrigeration; once open, it must be used within a day or two. It is good for making dips or ice creams. For most of the recipes in this book, use 'original' tofu, which is the equivalent of Chinese fresh tofu. Smoked tofu, which is specified in a few recipes, is also available.

WONTON WRAPPERS
These are squares of very thin pastry, like lasagne but much thinner. They measure about 7 cm (3 inches) each way, and can be bought from Chinese, Malaysian and Thai shops. They can be bought either fresh or frozen; their life in the refrigerator is limited to a few days.

If you freeze them, pack them in small packets (say, 125 g or 4 oz in a packet). Before you use them, thaw them completely, peeling each one off the pile before use. Remember, though, that they dry out very quickly and become brittle. Fillo pastry is a good alternative for most of the dishes that use wonton skins.

WATER SPINACH
Sometimes called 'swamp cabbage', this grows in South-East Asia as watercress does here. The taste is somewhere between watercress and spinach. Trim and clean it just as you do watercress, and cook it as you would spinach – you can eat it raw, but lightly cooked is better.

YARD-LONG BEANS
These can now be found in Thai and other ethnic shops, flown in once a week from Bangkok. They are very good when really fresh. To test the freshness, break a bean with your fingers; if it snaps easily it is fresh and young. A three-day-old bean will be stringy and will have to be cut with a knife. Young french beans can be substituted for yard-long beans, although the two flavours are quite different.

SOUPS

Soup is usually on the table throughout the meal. It takes the place of sauce and gravy, accompanying rice and other meat or fish dishes which have no sauce of their own. It helps, like a drink, to wash the food down. Thais, Indonesians and Malaysians, particularly the women, do not as a rule drink wine or beer; and I think most of them would agree with my grandmother, who used to tell me that drinking water and eating rice at the same time will make you feel instantly full, so you won't enjoy the meal in front of you.

A number of the soups in this section are quite substantial, and can be served as complete meals by themselves. And if you don't fancy having soup all through the meal, because by the end it has become stone cold, serve a small quantity of soup as a first course, or in the middle of a dinner with more than three courses, to act as an appetiser for what follows.

KAENG LIANG FAK THONG

Pumpkin soup with sweet basil	Serves 4–6

Preparation and cooking time: 50 minutes

1 kg (2 lb) pumpkin, peeled, de-seeded and cut into 2.5 cm (1-inch) cubes

125 g (4 oz) creamed coconut, chopped

¼ teaspoon ground white pepper

1 tablespoon fish sauce

For the stock:

1.2 litres (2 pints) cold water

1 small onion

5 cm (2-inch) piece of lemon grass

Pumpkin and sweet basil go excellently together: try this soup even if you don't like pumpkin pie! I have tried several versions, and this one is the easiest to make. Use either a whole small pumpkin or a segment of a large one. For this recipe, I approve of the use of creamed coconut. If you don't want your soup to look oriental, liquidise it and serve as a creamy golden soup, with chopped fresh basil leaves sprinkled on top.

Put all the ingredients for the stock in a large pan. Bring to the boil and simmer for 30 minutes. Then strain the stock into another saucepan.

Add the pumpkin cubes and cook for 8 minutes. Add the creamed coconut, and stir until it has all dissolved. Continue to simmer for

2.5 cm (1-inch) piece of fresh galingale, peeled	2 more minutes, then add the white pepper and fish sauce, and taste. Add more salt if necessary,
6 sweet basil leaves, plus extra to garnish	and put in extra basil leaves. Serve hot, immediately.
½ teaspoon salt, plus extra if necessary	

LAKSA LEMAK

Rice vermicelli soup with chicken and prawns   Serves 4–8

Preparation time: 45 minutes + 45 minutes cooking

1 small chicken

900 ml (1½ pints) water

500 g (1 lb) raw prawns with shells

½ teaspoon salt

2 tablespoons vegetable oil

3 shallots or 1 onion, sliced

2 garlic cloves, crushed

1–2 dried red chillies

2.5 cm (1-inch) piece of fresh ginger, peeled and chopped finely

1 teaspoon ground coriander

a large pinch of turmeric

175 g (6 oz) rice vermicelli

450 ml (¾ pint) very thick coconut milk (page 10)

salt and pepper

For the garnish:

125 g (4 oz) bean sprouts, blanched

3 tablespoons finely sliced spring onions

125 g (4 oz) fried tofu, sliced thinly (optional)

Cut the chicken into four and boil it in the water in a large saucepan for 45 minutes.

While the chicken is boiling, peel the prawns but do not discard the shells – wash them thoroughly and put them aside to be used later. De-vein the prawns, wash them, and dry with kitchen paper. Put the prawns in a bowl, rub them with ½ teaspoon of salt and keep in the fridge until needed.

After 45 minutes cooking, take the chicken out of the pan. Allow to cool and then separate the meat from the bones and skin and cut the meat into small pieces. Put the chicken pieces in the fridge and put the bones and skin back into the saucepan; continue simmering while you are preparing the rest of the soup.

Heat the oil in a frying-pan, and fry the shallots or onion, garlic, chillies and ginger for 2 minutes, stirring all the time. Add the prawn shells, the coriander and turmeric, stir again and add this mixture to the chicken stock in the pan; continue to simmer for 15 minutes. Then strain this stock through a strainer lined with muslin into another saucepan. If you make this stock a few hours or a day in advance, refrigerate it and skim off the fat before you assemble the soup, ready to serve.

Put the rice vermicelli in a large bowl and pour in enough boiling water to cover it. Cover the bowl and leave for 3 minutes, then strain off the water. Keep the vermicelli warm.

To assemble the soup, first heat the stock until it is just warm, add the coconut milk, and gently bring this to the boil. Stir, and while it is still boiling add the prawns and simmer for 2 minutes. Then add the chicken pieces. Continue to simmer for another 2 minutes, stirring most of the time. Divide the garnish among four or eight bowls, add the vermicelli in equal amounts to the bowls, then ladle the hot soup into the bowls, with the chicken pieces and prawns equally divided among them. Serve immediately.

SUP JAGUNG MUDA DENGAN TAHU

Baby corn and tofu soup   Serves 4–6

Preparation time: 25 minutes + 40–50 minutes cooking

For the vegetable stock:

1 tablespoon olive oil

1 teaspoon granulated sugar

3 shallots or 1 onion, chopped

1 garlic clove, chopped (optional)

1 small dried red chilli (optional)

5 cm (2-inch) piece of fresh ginger, peeled and chopped roughly

1 medium-size carrot, washed and cut into chunks

the stalks from the spinach

1.5 litres (2½ pints) water

To finish the soup:

375 g (12 oz) baby sweetcorn, sliced thinly

200 g (7 oz) smoked tofu, cut into 1 cm (½-inch) cubes

10–12 spinach leaves (or more), shredded roughly

salt and pepper

At home, in Indonesia, when I was a small girl, I remember having sweetcorn soup with spinach at least once a week because it was generally considered to be nourishing and healthy. Here I add smoked tofu, which gives the soup a lovely smoky flavour and a good contrast of textures: the baby corn crunchy and sweet, the smoked tofu soft and slightly salty. In this recipe the spinach is used only as a garnish.

Heat the oil in a saucepan, and add the sugar. Stir for 2 minutes, then add the rest of the ingredients for the stock, except the water. Stir these around for 2 minutes and then add the water. Bring to the boil and simmer for 30–40 minutes. Strain the stock into another saucepan, and discard the solids. This stock can be prepared well in advance.

About 10 minutes before you are going to serve the soup, heat the clear stock until it is just boiling, and add the baby corn and smoked tofu. Let this simmer for 6–8 minutes, adjust the seasoning, and add the spinach. Leave the soup to simmer for 10 seconds, and serve immediately.

SOTO AYAM

Mildly spiced Indonesian chicken soup   Serves 4–8

Preparation time: 30 minutes + 1 hour 25 minutes cooking

1.5 litres (2½ pints) water

1 small chicken, cut into 4

1 teaspoon salt

For the paste:

6 shallots or 1 large onion, chopped

3 garlic cloves, chopped

2.5 cm (1-inch) piece of fresh ginger, peeled and chopped

3 candlenuts or 5 blanched almonds, chopped

¼ teaspoon turmeric

½ teaspoon chilli powder

2 tablespoons groundnut or olive oil

2 tablespoons hot water

For the garnish:

4–5 tablespoons cooked rice (optional)

125 g (4 oz) bean sprouts, rinsed

1 tablespoon chopped fresh flat-leaf parsley

1 tablespoon chopped spring onion

4–8 lemon slices

2 tablespoons Goreng Bawang (Crispy fried shallots, page 78)

Like Laksa Lemak (Rice vermicelli soup with chicken and prawns, page 17), Soto Ayam is a substantial soup that can be eaten as a meal by itself with rice, to serve four, or just as a starter, in which case it serves eight. The difference is that Soto Ayam is made just with chicken and without coconut milk. It makes a meal by itself if you add plain boiled rice to the individual soup bowls.

Heat the water in a large pan until it is boiling. Put in the chicken pieces and the salt. Simmer for 50 minutes.

Put all the ingredients for the paste into a blender and blend for a few seconds only. Transfer this rough paste into a bowl and keep aside.

When the meat is cooked, strain off the stock from the pan and keep it for later. When cool enough to handle, shred the meat into small pieces, and throw away any fat but keep the bones.

Put the paste from the bowl into a clean saucepan, heat and stir all the time for 3 minutes. Add the chicken bones and half of the stock. Cover the pan and let it simmer for 15 minutes.

Strain the stock into another saucepan, and add the other half of the stock. Simmer the stock for 15 minutes, skimming if necessary. Put in the chicken meat and continue to simmer for another 5 minutes. Adjust the seasoning.

To serve, if this is to be a one-dish meal, put some boiled rice into the bowls. Divide the garnish (except the fried shallots) among the bowls, then ladle the hot soup and the chicken pieces into them. Sprinkle each bowl with fried shallots, and serve immediately.

KAI TOM KA

Chicken and galingale soup with coconut milk   Serves 4–6

Preparation time: 40 minutes + 45 minutes cooking

For the stock:

2 large chicken breasts, on the bone

1.2 litres (2 pints) cold water

4 lemon grass, washed and bruised

10 cm (4-inch) piece of galingale, peeled and sliced

4 kaffir lime leaves

3 shallots or 1 medium-size onion, sliced

3 small dried red chillies

To finish the soup:

125 g (4 oz) fresh shiitake or oyster mushrooms, sliced thinly

4 tablespoons lime juice or lemon juice

This soup should be quite hot and aromatic. Naturally, for the best results you should use fresh lemon grass, galingale and coriander leaves, and coconut milk made from freshly grated or desiccated coconut.

Tom Yam Koong (Hot and sour soup with prawns)

Soto Ayam (Mildly spiced Indonesian chicken soup)

1 tablespoon fish sauce

a large pinch of chilli powder

125 ml (4 fl oz) very thick coconut milk (page 10)

3 tablespoons chopped fresh basil

salt to taste

Put all the ingredients for the stock in a saucepan, boil for 15 minutes, then take out the chicken breasts. Bone and skin the breasts, slice them thinly and keep them aside. Put the bones and the skin back into the stockpot and continue cooking the stock for 30 minutes more.

Strain the stock through a fine sieve into another saucepan. You should have about 900 ml (1½ pints). Bring it back to the boil, add the chicken, mushrooms and the rest of the ingredients, except the coconut milk and basil. Simmer the mixture for 3 minutes, adjust the seasoning, and add the coconut milk. Simmer gently for 3 more minutes, stirring most of the time, to prevent the coconut milk from boiling. Just before serving, put the basil into the very hot soup, to cook it just a little. Serve hot, with the chicken breast and mushrooms divided equally among the soup bowls.

Kai Tom Ka (Chicken and galingale soup with coconut milk)

TOM YAM KOONG

Hot and sour soup with prawns   Serves 4–6

Preparation and cooking time: 1 hour

500 g (1 lb) large, raw prawns, with shells

½ teaspoon salt

125 g (4 oz) watercress

50 g (2 oz) oyster or button mushrooms

2 tablespoons chopped fresh coriander leaves

1 tablespoon fish sauce

For the stock:

1.2 litres (2 pints) cold water

3 tamarind slices

2–4 small dried red chillies

2 kaffir lime leaves

2.5 cm (1-inch) piece of fresh ginger, peeled

5 cm (2-inch) piece of fresh or dried galingale

1 stalk of fresh lemon grass, cut into 3

1 medium-size onion, chopped

½ teaspoon salt

600 ml (1 pint) strong but clear chicken or vegetable stock, or water, if necessary

This is the most popular of the Thai hot and sour soups. The stock should always be clear and transparent. The soup doesn't need to be too sour or too hot. The sourness should come from tamarind, but I often use a very good chicken stock and put in the juice of one lemon just before serving. What follows, however, is the authentic way of making hot and sour soup.

Peel and de-vein the prawns. Wash the prawns, and the shells, very thoroughly. Put the prawns on a plate, sprinkle with ½ teaspoon salt and keep in the fridge until needed. Reserve the shells.

Put the water into a large saucepan with the prawn shells and all the ingredients for the stock except the extra liquid. Bring this to the boil and simmer for 20–30 minutes. By this time the stock will be very fragrant from the lemon grass and other aromatic ingredients. Strain the stock through a fine sieve, or a sieve lined with muslin, into another large saucepan. Discard the solids. Add the extra stock or water, if used (this additional liquid is needed if the soup is to serve six people). Keep aside to reheat later.

While the hot and sour stock is brewing, prepare the vegetables. Pick the watercress leaves off the stems as you wash them. Shred the oyster mushrooms, or slice the button mushrooms finely. Put the clear, strained stock back on the stove; turn the heat up and bring the stock to a rolling boil, then add the prawns, mushrooms and coriander leaves. Let the mixture boil for 3 minutes, add the watercress and the fish sauce. Cook the soup for just *one* more minute, then serve immediately.

APPETISERS AND SAVOURY SNACKS

The climate and the life-styles of Thailand, Indonesia and Malaysia are very favourable to casual eating outdoors. I mean casual, because any elaborately planned picnic or barbecue party tends to become unmanageably large; the custom of the extended family will not allow you to exclude even the remotest cousin. Admittedly, this means there are plenty of people to help with the preparation and the cooking. But you can imagine what sort of gathering you will have when three or four generations assemble.

Street food vendors and food bazaars flourish. Promenade eating is always in fashion: everywhere you will see groups of young people, with or without their parents, strolling along the high streets and the bazaars in their best clothes, intending to see and be seen by friends and acquaintances. There is a tremendous variety of finger food. I dream of devoting a whole book to street food some day, before it is overwhelmed by the fast-food chains. However, never mind the dream for now. Here are some recipes based on the street food I love so much, for you to recreate and serve as appetisers with drinks or as a first course.

PRIK YAI SAI MOO

Stuffed peppers with pork   Makes 16

Preparation and cooking time: 35 minutes + chilling

4 peppers (red, yellow,
green and orange), de-
seeded and quartered

2 large eggs (size 2), beaten
lightly

150 ml (¼ pint) sunflower
or corn oil

some salad leaves

For the filling:

500 g (1 lb) minced pork

1 teaspoon each finely sliced
lemon grass, basil, and
kaffir lime leaves, or finely
chopped thyme, tarragon
and parsley

1 red chilli, de-seeded and
chopped finely, or ¾
teaspoon chilli powder

*This will give you a plateful of brightly-coloured
starters and a chance to use your home-grown herbs.
Don't be too carried away, though; three different
herbs is, I suggest, the most you should use, otherwise
you'll spoil the taste of the dish. Familiar herbs
can be used here as alternatives to the
Thai fragrant herbs of lemon grass,
basil and kaffir lime leaves.*

*Siu Mai (Steamed won ton
with prawns and chicken)*

2 tablespoons finely
chopped spring onions

2 garlic cloves, chopped
finely

1 tablespoon fish sauce or
light soy sauce

1 teaspoon granulated
sugar

Martabak (Savoury won ton with beef filling)

*Prik Yai Sai Moo
(Stuffed peppers with pork)*

Blanch the peppers in boiling water for 1
minute, drain and refresh them in cold water.
Put them in a colander, and pat dry with some
kitchen paper. Keep aside.

Put all the ingredients for the filling in a glass
bowl, mix them with a wooden spoon (or knead
them by hand until they are all well mixed). Fill
the pepper segments with the filling, and chill
them for 30 minutes.

Just before frying them, roll them in the
beaten egg. Heat the oil, preferably in a wok or a
wide non-stick shallow saucepan. When the oil
is hot, fry the stuffed peppers, 4 pieces at a time,
stuffed-side down, for 2 minutes. Then turn
them over and continue frying for another 2
minutes. Turn them over once more and fry for
1 more minute. Take them out with a slotted
spoon and drain on a plate lined with absorbent
kitchen paper. Serve hot or cold on a plate lined
with the salad leaves.

MARTABAK

Savoury won ton with beef filling   Makes 20–25

Preparation and cooking time: about 1 hour + cooling

175 g (6 oz) packet of won
ton skins, or 40–50 7 cm
(3-inch) fillo pastry squares

300 ml (½ pint) sunflower
or corn oil

For the filling:

2 tablespoons olive oil

2 large onions, sliced finely

2 garlic cloves, chopped
finely

5 cm (2-inch) piece of fresh
ginger, peeled and chopped
finely

1 teaspoon ground coriander

½ teaspoon ground cumin

½ teaspoon turmeric or
curry powder

5 cm (2-inch) piece of lemon
grass, outer leaves
discarded, chopped finely

1 teaspoon salt

500 g (1 lb) lean minced
beef

4 spring onions, chopped
finely

3 eggs, beaten

*This is one of the most popular street foods in
Indonesia, especially in the open-air evening markets.
It is easy to make and will be very popular at parties.*

Heat the olive oil in a wok or frying-pan and fry
the onions, garlic and ginger until they are soft.
Add the other filling ingredients, except the
minced beef, spring onions and eggs. Fry for
another half-minute, stirring all the time, and
add the meat. Mix well and fry, stirring
occasionally, for about 15 minutes. Let the
mixture cool for 30 minutes to an hour. Put the
mixture in a bowl, add the chopped spring
onions and mix well.

When you are ready to cook the Martabak,
add the beaten eggs to the filling and mix well.
Lay a few won ton skins on a flat plate or tray.
Put a tablespoonful of filling into each won ton
square. Then put another square on top, and
press the edges down so that they are more or
less sealed.

Put the sunflower or corn oil into a frying-pan
and heat it to a high temperature. Fry the filled
Martabak for about 2 minutes each side: turn
once only. The casing should be quite crisp
around the edges, but not in the middle, and the
finished Martabak should be flat and evenly
filled with meat almost to the edge. Serve hot
or cold.

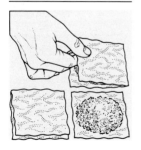

SIU MAI

Steamed won ton with prawns and chicken   Makes 50–55

Preparation time: 15–20 minutes + 30 minutes chilling +
15 minutes cooking

250 g (8 oz) won ton skins

For the filling:

*500 g (1 lb) peeled raw
prawns, de-veined, and
chopped or minced coarsely*

*500 g (1 lb) skinned chicken
breast, minced finely*

1 teaspoon salt

*75 g (3 oz) fresh shiitake or
button mushrooms, chopped*

1 teaspoon sugar

*¾ teaspoon ground white
pepper*

2 tablespoons light soy sauce

*2 tablespoons finely
chopped spring onions*

1 egg white, beaten lightly

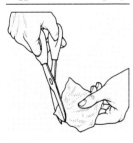

*This is definitely a Chinese dish, made with prawns
and pork, but popular with everybody in Malaysia
and Indonesia. Those who do not eat pork will make
their Siu Mai with chicken. For me, the combination
of prawns and chicken is as good as prawns and pork.*

Put the prawns and chicken in a large glass bowl,
add the salt and mix well, either by kneading
with your hand or by stirring with a wooden
spoon. Then add all the other filling ingredients,
and stir them well into the prawn and chicken
mixture. Cling-film the bowl and chill for at
least 30 minutes.

When you are ready to stuff the Siu Mai, first
cut off, with a pair of scissors, the four corners of
the won ton skins (1). Put 1 tablespoon of the
filling in the centre of the first won ton skin and
gather the edges to make a bag. Lift this onto the
palm of your hand, then squeeze it gently in the
middle as if to make a waist in the filled won ton
(2). Open up the bag at the top, and press the
filling down with a small spoon that has been
wetted with cold water, so as to make the surface
of the filling flat.

When the Siu Mai are ready to cook, steam
them in a bamboo steamer for 8–10 minutes. If
you don't have a bamboo steamer, put them on
an oiled plate. Put a trivet or a soup plate upside
down at the bottom of a large saucepan, and fill
the saucepan with hot water up to the top of the
trivet (or plate). Then put the plate of Siu Mai on
top. Bring the water to the boil, cover the
saucepan and cook for 12–15 minutes.

Serve hot as a starter, accompanied by a sweet
chilli sauce such as Nam Jeem (page 74), if you
wish.

PERGEDEL JAGUNG

Savoury sweetcorn fritters   Makes 20–25

Preparation and cooking time: about 40 minutes

325 g (11½ oz) can of sweetcorn	*In Indonesia fresh sweetcorn, grilled while you wait, is a favourite snack. You can buy it in the market, or wait for the vendor to come and grill it in front of your house. Corn fritters are also popular and very easy to make, especially if, as I suggest here, you use canned sweetcorn.*
4 shallots or 1 medium-size onion, chopped finely	
1 red chilli, de-seeded and chopped, or ½ teaspoon chilli powder	
2 garlic cloves, chopped finely	Drain the canned sweetcorn and put it into a bowl, then mash it a little with a spoon just to break the kernels so they won't pop when fried.
1 teaspoon ground coriander	Alternatively, put the corn into a blender and blend for a few seconds. Then mix it with all the
2 tablespoons chopped spring onions	other ingredients except the oil. Taste, and add more salt if necessary.
3 tablespoons rice flour or plain flour	Heat the oil in a wok or frying-pan. Drop a heaped teaspoonful of the mixture into the pan.
1 teaspoon baking powder	Flatten it with a fork, and repeat this process until you have 5 or 6 fritters in the pan. Each one
salt to taste	should fry for about 3 minutes on each side, and should be turned over only once. Serve hot or
1 large egg	cold as a snack with drinks, or as finger food.
125 ml (4 fl oz) oil	

KHAI TUN

Steamed egg   Serves 4

Preparation time: 10 minutes + 8–25 minutes cooking

8 large eggs (size 2), beaten lightly	*There are many variations of this dish, depending on who you are going to serve it to: children, or maybe somebody who is recovering from illness, or yourself when you want a quick lunch or a snack. My own version is usually made with some leftovers of Chiang Rai (Spicy minced pork, page 60).*
2 tablespoons chopped spring onions	
1 large red chilli, de-seeded and chopped finely, or a large pinch of chilli powder	
2 garlic cloves, chopped finely	

Pergedel Jagung (Savoury sweetcorn fritters)
Khai Tun (Steamed egg)

1 tablespoon fish sauce or light soy sauce	Put all the ingredients in a glass bowl and mix them thoroughly by stirring quickly with a large spoon for several seconds. Divide among four well-oiled or buttered ramekins or other suitable heatproof bowls. Steam in a steamer for 8 minutes. Alternatively, you can cook them in a bain-marie in the oven at Gas Mark 4/180°C/350°F for 25–30 minutes. Serve warm or cold.
125 g (4 oz) shelled roughly chopped prawns, or chopped cooked chicken	
a few leaves of fresh basil or mint	
2 tablespoons coconut cream (page 10), or single cream	
oil or butter for greasing	
salt and pepper to taste	

TANG TONG

Golden bags   Makes 20–24

Preparation and cooking time: about 30 minutes

125 g (4 oz) won ton skins, or 125 g (4 oz) fillo pastry	*In Thailand these are traditionally made with dried tofu sheets, but in this country won ton skins or fillo pastry can be used.*
24 chives, about 10 cm (5 inches) long, blanched	
sunflower or corn oil for deep-frying	Cut the won ton skins or fillo pastry into 7 cm (3-inch) squares, stack them on a plate, cover with cling film and refrigerate while you prepare the filling.
For the filling:	
125 g (4 oz) lean pork, minced finely	Put all the ingredients for the filling in a bowl and mix well with a wooden spoon or with your hand, kneading them slightly. Divide into 20–24 portions, and put each portion in the middle of a won ton skin or fillo pastry square; gather the four corners of the wrapper and tie the bag with the chive just above the filling.
125 g (4 oz) shelled raw prawns, chopped	
50 g (2 oz) water chestnuts, chopped	
2 tablespoons chopped spring onions	
2 garlic cloves, chopped finely	Heat the oil in a wok or saucepan and deep-fry the Tang Tong, 5 or 6 at a time, for 2–3 minutes.
5 cm (2-inch) piece of fresh ginger, peeled and chopped finely	

Serve hot or warm with Nam Jeem (A sweet chilli sauce, page 74) as a dip.

2 tablespoons chopped fresh coriander leaves (optional)
1 tablespoon fish sauce or light soy sauce

¾ teaspoon ground white
pepper

1 egg (size 2), beaten
lightly

KHAI KWAM

Eggs stuffed with prawns and crabmeat   Makes 8

Preparation and cooking time: 45 minutes

4 eggs (size 2), boiled for 4–
5 minutes

For the stuffing:

125 g (4 oz) peeled raw
prawns, minced

50 g (2 oz) cooked crabmeat
(white meat only)

1 tablespoon chopped fresh
coriander leaves

1 tablespoon chopped fresh
chives or spring onions

2 garlic cloves, chopped
finely

a large pinch of chilli
powder

1 tablespoon fish sauce

1 tablespoon chopped
creamed coconut

3 tablespoons hot water

For the batter:

75 g (3 oz) plain flour

150 ml (¼ pint) warm
water

1 tablespoon olive oil

a large pinch of salt

300 ml (½ pint) vegetable
oil

*These Thai stuffed eggs are usually made with duck
eggs, and they are called* khai kwam, *meaning
'upside-down eggs', because when you are deep-frying
them the filled half will be downwards. Served with a
salad dressed with vinaigrette, these make a good first-
course dish.*

Peel and halve the eggs. Scrape out the yolks and
put them in a bowl. Keep the halved egg-whites
aside. Mash the yolks with a fork and mix them
well with all the ingredients for the stuffing.

Fill the halved egg-whites with the stuffing
and mound it up to make the egg shape. (You
can prepare them up to 24 hours in advance and
store them in the fridge.)

To make the batter, put the flour, warm
water, olive oil and salt in a bowl, and beat until
smooth.

Dip the stuffed eggs in the batter and deep-fry
in batches in the hot vegetable oil (180°C/350°F)
for 3–4 minutes or until golden-brown. Keep
the filling downwards while frying. Take the
eggs out with a slotted spoon and drain on
kitchen paper. They can be served hot, warm or
cold.

SATAYS AND OTHER MARINATED AND GRILLED DISHES

Satays are meat or seafood on skewers – like kebabs but smaller. They are popular all over South-East Asia, but each country has its favourite marinades.

If you need to brush some of the marinade on your meat or fish while it is grilling, instead of a nylon brush use a bunch of herbs such as thyme or rosemary, or best of all a stick of fresh lemon grass. Just cut off and discard about 1 cm (½ inch) from the hard root-end of the lemon grass, and beat the cut end of the stem, not too hard, with the handle of a knife or a steak hammer until you get a flexible lemon grass brush. This will add a lovely aroma to your cooking, and no smell of melting nylon!

SATÉ AYAM

Chicken satays   As a main course serves 4–6

Preparation and cooking time: 30–40 minutes + marinating

1 kg (2 lb) chicken breast and thigh meat, cut into 1 cm (½-inch) cubes

For the marinade:

3 shallots or 1 small onion, sliced finely

2 garlic cloves, sliced finely

1 teaspoon ground coriander

¾ teaspoon ground cumin

½ teaspoon chilli powder

2.5 cm (1-inch) piece of fresh ginger, peeled and chopped finely

2 tablespoons light soy sauce

If I want to be very quick in preparing this I use only skinned chicken breasts, but these can taste rather dry. So for taste, it is better to use the thigh meat as well, which you can purchase already boned and skinned. If you are using bamboo skewers, soak them first in cold water for at least 2 hours or overnight, then rinse and dry them. Metal skewers are more practical to use, because it is easier to slide the meat or fish on and off them.

Mix all the ingredients for the marinade in a glass bowl. Put the meat in and mix well to ensure that all the pieces are well coated with the marinade. Refrigerate for at least 2 hours, or better still marinate in the fridge overnight.

When ready to grill, put the pieces onto 12 short bamboo skewers or 6 metal ones. Grill on

32

1 tablespoon groundnut oil

1 tablespoon distilled malt vinegar or lemon juice

½ teaspoon salt

1 teaspoon brown sugar

charcoal or under an electric or gas grill for 3–5 minutes each side.

For serving suggestions, see Satay Daging (Beef satays), below.

SATAY DAGING

Beef satays   Serves 4–6

Preparation and cooking time: 30–40 minutes + marinating

1 kg (2 lb) rump steak or topside or silverside, beaten and cut into 2 cm (¾-inch) pieces

For the marinade:

4 shallots or 1 medium-size onion, sliced finely

3 garlic cloves, sliced finely

1 tablespoon coriander seeds, dry-roasted and crushed roughly

½ teaspoon ground cumin

½ teaspoon chilli powder

¾ teaspoon coarsely ground black pepper

5 cm (2-inch) piece of fresh ginger, peeled and chopped finely

2 tablespoons light soy sauce

1 tablespoon groundnut or olive oil

1 tablespoon white distilled malt vinegar or lemon juice

½ teaspoon salt

1 teaspoon brown sugar

1 tablespoon whisky (optional)

The best cut to use here is rump steak, but if you are using a less tender one, such as topside or silverside, my suggestion is to add one tablespoonful of whisky to the marinade. This is definitely not a Malaysian custom, but just a practical tip to make the beef more tender! Whatever cut you use, it is a good idea to beat the slab of meat with the flat side of a large knife or with a wooden mallet to flatten it well before you cut it up.

Mix all the ingredients for the marinade in a glass bowl, and mix in the pieces of meat. Refrigerate for at least 2 hours or overnight. Just before you are ready to grill, put the meat onto 12 bamboo skewers or 4–6 metal skewers. Grill for 3 minutes each side. Turn over once. Serve hot with peanut sauce (Sambal Kacang, page 76).

Serving suggestions for satays:

As a cocktail snack: (serves 15–20) put individual pieces of meat on cocktail sticks and serve the peanut sauce as a dip. *As a first course*: (serves 8) serve on the skewers, or strip the meat off the skewers onto a bed of lettuce leaves with the peanut sauce poured over the meat, and a sprinkling of crisp fried onions if wished. *As a main course*: serve on a bed of hot plain boiled rice or fried rice (Nasi Goreng, page 87) or cold compressed rice (Lontong, page 83), on or off the skewers, with the peanut sauce poured over the meat and everything sprinkled with crispy fried shallots (Goreng Bawang, page 78). *Pictured on page 4.*

SATAY IKAN LAUT

Mixed grill of seafish   Serves 4–6

Preparation and cooking time: about 30 minutes + marinating

375 g (12 oz) tuna steaks, cut into 2 cm (¾-inch) cubes

375 g (12 oz) salmon steaks, cut into 2 cm (¾-inch) cubes

375 g (12 oz) monk fish, cut into 2 cm (¾-inch) cubes

For the marinade:

2 tablespoons lemon juice

2 tablespoons olive oil

½ teaspoon chilli powder

2 tablespoons light soy sauce

2 shallots or 1 small onion, sliced finely

2 garlic cloves, sliced finely

½ teaspoon salt

2 teaspoons brown sugar

3 kaffir lime or 2 bay leaves

For the piquant sauce:

2 small fresh chillies, chopped finely, or ½ teaspoon chilli powder

3 garlic cloves, chopped finely

1 teaspoon sugar

1 tablespoon white distilled vinegar

2 tablespoons light soy sauce

2 tablespoons hot water

1 tablespoon olive oil

3 tablespoons coarsely ground roasted or fried peanuts

For fish satays the marinade is very simple. I also give an alternative piquant sauce to the usual peanut sauce. Use any combination of firm-fleshed fish – the thing to be fussy about here is that the fish steaks you buy should be very fresh. I find I have more satisfactory results by using metal skewers. You may have wondered about the alternative spellings satay *and* saté. *The former is the Malaysian spelling and the latter is used in Indonesia. I have used both, according to the country of origin of the various recipes.*

Mix well all the ingredients for the marinade and divide it among 3 small glass bowls. Marinate each kind of fish separately. Refrigerate overnight.

Just before grilling, put the fish onto metal skewers, 2 pieces of each fish on each skewer. Grill them for 3 minutes, turn over and continue grilling for another 3 minutes.

Mix all the ingredients for the sauce in a glass bowl and serve as a dip with the hot grilled fish satays. You can eat these fish satays with rice, potatoes or pasta, and a green salad or plain boiled or steamed vegetables.

GRADOOK MOO NUENG TOW JEOW

Steamed and grilled spare ribs with black bean sauce Serves 4

Preparation time: 15 minutes + marinating + 60–65 minutes cooking

1 kg (2 lb) pork spare ribs, cut into about 7 cm (3-inch) pieces

For the marinade:

4 tablespoons fermented black beans, soaked in cold water for 6 minutes and drained

5 cm (2-inch) piece of fresh ginger, peeled and chopped

4 garlic cloves, chopped

2 large red chillies, chopped, or ½ teaspoon chilli powder

2 teaspoons brown sugar

1 tablespoon light soy sauce

2 tablespoons lemon juice

2 tablespoons peanut oil

2 tablespoons cold water

Fermented black beans are available, packed dry in cardboard containers, from oriental grocers. You need to rinse the beans first, then soak them in cold water for 6 minutes to soften them. This dish, like so many other steamed dishes from South-East Asia, will taste better if it is either fried or grilled after steaming. This is my favourite for a large barbecue party, because the marinating and steaming of the spare ribs can be done well in advance and the grilling takes only a few minutes.

Put all the ingredients for the marinade into a blender, and blend until smooth. Transfer the marinade to a large glass bowl, and add the spare ribs. Mix until all the spare ribs are well coated with the marinade. Refrigerate for 2 hours, or overnight.

Put the spare ribs in a dish that will fit your steamer, and steam them for 40–45 minutes.

If you don't have a steamer, use a large saucepan: put a plate upside-down in the saucepan, and put the plate full of spare ribs on top. Add hot water to reach halfway up to the spare ribs plate (but, of course, don't let it overflow onto the ribs). Bring the water to the boil, cover the saucepan, and steam for 45 minutes.

Drain the meat, but do not throw away the cooking juice. It can be used to moisten the ribs again if you store them for longer than 24 hours before grilling them.

The ribs can be grilled straight away, or left to cool and refrigerated for up to 24 hours. To grill them, you need only 10 minutes, 5 minutes for each side. Serve hot with fried rice and vegetables, or just a salad.

AYAM PANGGANG KECAP

Roasted and grilled chicken   Serves 4

Preparation time: 10 minutes + 60 minutes roasting + marinating + 10 minutes grilling

1 free-range chicken, weighing about 1.75 kg (4 lb)

2 tablespoons lemon juice

½ teaspoon salt

2 tablespoons soft butter

For the marinade:

3 garlic cloves, peeled and crushed

½ teaspoon chilli powder

1 teaspoon shrimp paste (optional)

1 teaspoon ground coriander

1 tablespoon lemon juice

2 tablespoons light soy sauce

2 teaspoons demerara sugar

1 tablespoon groundnut or olive oil

This recipe, popular in Malaysia and Indonesia, is ideal for picnics and barbecues. It is only mildly spicy, and tastes equally good either cold or hot. It can be prepared well in advance for last-minute grilling.

Preheat the oven to Gas Mark 5/190°C/375°F. Rub the chicken with the lemon juice, salt and soft butter. Roast it for 1¼ hours, and leave it to cool.

When it is cool enough to touch, cut the chicken in half. Clean the inside by taking out the ribs and neck bones; wipe the chicken with kitchen paper, then beat it gently on the inside with a small rolling pin or a wooden mallet to break the meat but not the skin.

Mix all the ingredients for the marinade in a small glass bowl. Then, with your hand, rub the marinade all over the chicken, inside and out, and under the skin as far as you can. Leave in the fridge for a few hours or overnight. Grill it on charcoal or under an electric or gas grill for 4–5 minutes each side. Leave the skin side to be grilled last. Serve hot or cold.

Ayam Panggang Kecap (Roasted and grilled chicken)
Satay Ikan Laut (Mixed grill of seafish)

36

FISH AND SEAFOOD

I remember, as a child, the delight of everybody when they saw a large river-fish gasping for more water in a newly-planted paddy field. It was bad luck for the fish, I suppose, to be swept into the paddy field from the small irrigation canal, where, presumably, it thought it had found a calm place to breed, away from the stony shallows and tumbling water of the river. But it was a great find for whoever caught it; it would provide him and his family with a delicious evening meal and plenty of fresh protein.

Besides fresh-water fish, there is always a great quantity of seafood, for all these countries have long coastlines and a large proportion of the people live near the sea. No less desirable are dried fish. Drying the fish in the sun, with salt, was the only method I knew of in those days to preserve what was not sold and eaten on the day it was caught. Dried salted fish is just as important a part of most people's diet today.

Naturally, for the recipes in this section, I am assuming that you will do everything you can to get the freshest fish possible. I do approve, however, of using frozen uncooked large prawns, because, alas, these are the only uncooked prawns available where I live.

SAMBAL GORENG UDANG

Prawns in rich coconut-milk sauce   Serves 6–8

Preparation time: about 15 minutes + 20 minutes cooking

450 ml (¾ pint) hot water

5 cm (2-inch) piece of fresh lemon grass

2 kaffir lime, lemon or bay leaves

2 ripe tomatoes, peeled and chopped

125 g (4 oz) creamed coconut, chopped

1 kg (2 lb) frozen raw king prawns, thawed completely

For the paste:

3 shallots or 1 small onion, chopped

2 garlic cloves

5 cm (2-inch) piece of fresh ginger, peeled and sliced

3 large red chillies, de-seeded and chopped

1 teaspoon shrimp paste (optional)

1 teaspoon ground coriander

1 teaspoon paprika

½ teaspoon salt, plus extra to taste

1 tablespoon tamarind water (page 14) or lemon juice

2 tablespoons olive or groundnut oil

2 tablespoons cold water

Sambal goreng *is a generic name for dishes that are found all over Indonesia and Malaysia. The most popular of these is made with* udang, *which are prawns – fresh, uncooked king prawns. Large king prawns are now available from many supermarkets in the UK, peeled, de-veined, partially pre-cooked and frozen. Using prawns of this type will shorten the preparation time considerably, and as long as they are cooked for not more than 3 minutes they taste excellent.*

Put all the ingredients for the paste in a blender or food processor, and blend until smooth.

Put the paste in a saucepan, bring to the boil and stir continuously for 4 minutes. Add the hot water, lemon grass and kaffir lime, lemon or bay leaves. Bring back to the boil and let the mixture bubble gently for 20 minutes. Add the tomatoes and the creamed coconut and stir to dissolve the coconut. Simmer gently, stirring all the time, for 2 minutes. Adjust the seasoning. Up to this point the sauce can be made well in advance. It can be refrigerated for up to 24 hours, but not frozen.

Just before serving, put the sauce into a saucepan and bring it to a rolling boil. Stir, put in the prawns (which *must* be completely thawed), and simmer for 3 minutes only. Take out and discard the lemon grass and kaffir lime, lemon or bay leaves. Serve hot with Nasi Goreng (Fried rice, page 87) or any other kind of rice, accompanied by stir-fried vegetables or a salad. *Pictured on page 5.*

UDANG BUMBU ACAR

Prawns in piquant sauce   Serves 4

Preparation and cooking time: 20–25 minutes

16–20 raw king prawns, peeled and de-veined

½ teaspoon salt

6 tablespoons hot water

1 teaspoon brown sugar

2 tablespoons mild vinegar

2 tablespoons roughly chopped fresh mint

For the paste:

3 candlenuts

2 shallots or ½ onion, chopped

2 garlic cloves, chopped

2 small red or green chillies

5 cm (2-inch) piece of fresh ginger, peeled and chopped

½ teaspoon salt, plus extra if necessary

2 tablespoons cold water

2 tablespoons groundnut or olive oil

In many Asian countries acar *(the* c *is pronounced like* ch *in 'church') can mean vegetables and/or fruit that are slightly pickled, either to preserve them or to give them a sweet-and-sour or hot-and-sour taste. The sourness usually comes from lemon or lime juice or vinegar used in the cooking or in the pickle.* Bumbu acar *means 'cooked with ingredients usually used to make an* acar*'.*

Wash the prawns and pat them dry with kitchen paper. Put them in a glass bowl and rub them with the salt. Keep aside in a cool place or in the fridge while you are preparing the paste.

Put all the ingredients for the paste in a blender, and blend them until smooth. Put the paste in a wok or saucepan, heat and bring to the boil, then stir continuously for 4 minutes. Add the rest of the ingredients, except the prawns and mint. Continue cooking, stirring from time to time, for another 4 minutes. Taste, and adjust the seasoning. Bring the sauce to the boil again and put in the prawns, stir, and cook on a high heat for 3 minutes. Add the chopped mint, stir again and remove from the stove. Serve hot or cold as a first course. This can also be served as a main course with rice and any cooked vegetables or a salad.

Udang Bumbu Acar (Prawns in piquant sauce)

KARI KETAM

Crab curry   Serves 4

Preparation time: 20–25 minutes + 25–30 minutes cooking

2 medium-size crabs, or 2 dressed crabs

1.2 litres (2 pints) coconut milk (page 10)

For the crab cakes (optional):

2 garlic cloves, chopped finely

a pinch of salt

3 tablespoons rice or potato flour

1 large egg (size 2)

For the curry paste:

4 shallots or 1 onion, sliced

4 garlic cloves, chopped roughly

3 large red chillies, chopped roughly

5 cm (2-inch) piece of fresh ginger, peeled and sliced

2 teaspoons ground coriander

1/2 teaspoon ground cumin

1/2 teaspoon turmeric

a large pinch of ground nutmeg

5 cm (2-inch) piece of lemon grass, outer leaves discarded

2 tablespoons tamarind water (page 14)

1 teaspoon salt

In Malaysia crabs are usually cooked in the shells, cut up into four with the meat still inside. You can try asking the fish counter to do this for you, or you can just buy the fresh dressed crab. There is no doubt that fresh crab meat is superior to frozen or canned. Here I shall describe two ways of preparing this curry. First, the authentic Malaysian way; and second, by making the crab meat from the dressed crab into crab cakes, cooking the cakes in the curry sauce, and serving them piled inside the crab shell. Either way the curry sauce can be prepared well in advance.

If making crab cakes, mix the meat from the two dressed crabs with all the other ingredients for the crab cakes in a glass bowl. (Reserve the shells to serve the curry in.) Knead a little, then make into small balls; flatten them to make small round cakes. Keep them in the fridge until you are ready to use them.

If using whole crabs, clean them and cut them into four, and cut the claws into manageably-sized pieces.

Put all the ingredients for the curry paste in a blender or food processor with 3 tablespoons of the coconut milk, and blend until smooth. Transfer into a saucepan and bring to the boil. Stir continuously for 4 minutes. Add the remaining coconut milk, increase the heat and bring to the boil again. Stir again and turn down the heat a little. Simmer the sauce, stirring frequently, for 25–30 minutes or until the sauce has reduced by half. Adjust the seasoning. Up to this point the sauce can be prepared up to 24 hours in advance.

Just before serving, heat the sauce, bring to a rolling boil, put in the cut-up crabs or the crab cakes carefully, and simmer for 3–4 minutes. Serve hot with plain boiled rice and vegetables of your choice.

GULAI IKAN DENGAN KENTANG DAN KACANG PANJANG

Fish with potatoes and beans in coconut sauce   Serves 4–6

Preparation time: 30 minutes + 15–18 minutes cooking

1 litre (1¾ pints) coconut milk (page 10)

250 g (8 oz) new potatoes, scraped and halved

2 kaffir lime or bay leaves

2 tamarind slices

1 lemon grass stem, halved

375 g (12 oz) yard-long or french beans, cut into 5 cm (2-inch) lengths

1 kg (2 lb) cod or haddock fillets, cut into 10 cm (4-inch) squares

For the paste:

3 shallots or 1 small onion, sliced

2 garlic cloves

2 large red chillies, chopped roughly

5 cm (2-inch) piece of fresh ginger, peeled and chopped

2 teaspoons ground coriander

1 teaspoon turmeric

½ teaspoon salt

2 tablespoons cold water

2 tablespoons olive or peanut oil

Gulai is an Indonesian/Malay word for a dish with a lot of sauce, usually coconut sauce. We do not thicken this in any way; sometimes we reduce the sauce by cooking. We normally serve gulai *with rice in a deep dish or soup plate and eat it with a spoon. This is a one-dish meal, with potatoes and yard-long beans. Put more potatoes in if you don't want to eat the* gulai *with rice.*

Put all the ingredients for the paste into a blender and blend until smooth. Put the paste in a saucepan, and place it on a medium heat until the paste boils. Stir continuously with a wooden spoon for 4 minutes. Add half of the coconut milk, and bring the mixture back to the boil. Immediately it boils, stir, and add the potatoes and the kaffir lime or bay leaves, tamarind slices and lemon grass. Simmer for 15–18 minutes, stirring occasionally.

Add the remaining coconut milk, increase the heat and bring the mixture to the boil again. Stir, and add the beans. Continue cooking, stirring occasionally, for 3 minutes; then add the fish. Simmer for 6 minutes, adjust the seasoning and remove the aromatics. Serve hot.

IKAN MASAK TAUCO

Fish in yellow bean sauce

Serves 4–6

Preparation and cooking time: about 25 minutes

1 teaspoon ground white pepper

1 teaspoon granulated sugar

2 tablespoons plain flour

1 kg (2 lb) boneless haddock fillet, skinned and cut into 5 cm (2-inch) pieces

For the paste:

2 tablespoons yellow bean sauce

4 garlic cloves

5 cm (2-inch) piece of fresh ginger, peeled and chopped

½ teaspoon chilli powder

The fermented yellow beans used in this recipe are common to all three countries dealt with in this book. In Thailand they spell the name tow jeow, which is pronounced very like tauco in Indonesia and Malaysia. The beans are available in two colours, yellow and black; both are made from soya beans. More information about this ingredient will be found on page 11.

Gulai Ikan Dengan Kentang Dan Kacang Panjang (Fish with potatoes and beans in coconut sauce)

Yam Mamuang (Mango salad with monk fish)

1 tablespoon tamarind water
(page 14) or lemon juice

1 tablespoon tomato ketchup

To finish:

4 tablespoons groundnut oil

1 large onion, sliced finely

3 green chillies, de-seeded
and sliced finely

250 g (8 oz) small button
mushrooms, wiped and
sliced finely

1 teaspoon light soy sauce

4 tablespoons chopped
spring onions

Mix the pepper, sugar and flour and spread them
evenly on both sides of the fish. Leave the fish in
a cool place while you are preparing the rest of
the ingredients.

Put all the ingredients for the paste in a blender
or food processor. Blend them until smooth and
transfer them into a bowl.

Heat 3 tablespoons of the oil in a large non-
stick frying-pan. When hot add the sliced onion
and green chillies. Stir-fry this mixture until it is
slightly coloured, and add the fish pieces. Gently
turn them over several times until they are also
slightly coloured. This will take about 5
minutes.

Remove the fish, onions and chillies to a plate,
taking care that the oil is left in the pan. Add the
remaining 1 tablespoon of oil to the pan, add the
mushrooms, stir-fry for 2 minutes and add the
soy sauce. Keep stirring for another minute and
add the paste from the bowl. Let this simmer for
5 minutes, stirring almost all the time. Replace
the fish, onions and chillies, and stir again,
gently so as not to break up the fish. Continue
cooking on a low flame for 2 minutes. Add the
chopped spring onions, cook for 1 minute more
and serve hot with plain boiled rice or boiled
potatoes and a salad.

*Ikan Masak Tauco
(Fish in yellow
bean sauce)*

KOONG TORD

Marinated and fried prawns　　　　　　　　　　　　　　　Serves 4–6

Preparation time: 30 minutes + marinating + 6–9 minutes cooking

*1 kg (2 lb) raw king
prawns, peeled, with tails*

*450 ml (¾ pint) groundnut
or sunflower oil*

For the marinade:

*125 g (4 oz) creamed
coconut, chopped*

250 ml (8 fl oz) hot water

*2.5 cm (1-inch) piece of
fresh galingale, chopped, or
½ teaspoon laos powder*

*5 cm (2-inch) piece of lemon
grass, outer leaves
discarded, chopped*

5 coriander roots, chopped

3 shallots, chopped

2 garlic cloves, chopped

2 small fresh or dried chillies

1 tablespoon lemon juice

1 teaspoon salt

*There are several Indonesian ways of frying prawns
which are delicious but quite time-consuming to make.
Here is another way, from Thailand, that gives you
the subtle taste of the marinade, yet is quick to prepare
and really delicious. The marinating can be done 2–4
hours in advance.*

Put all the ingredients for the marinade in a
blender or food processor and blend them until
smooth. Transfer them to a glass bowl and allow
to cool. Split each prawn lengthways, but leave
the two halves joined at the tail; this will make
them open out like butterflies when you fry
them. Mix them into the marinade. Keep
refrigerated for at least 2 hours, or as long as you
like up to 4 hours.

When ready to fry, drain the excess marinade
from the prawns by putting them in a colander.
Heat the oil in a wok or deep-fryer, and fry the
prawns in two or three batches, each batch for
3 minutes only.

Serve hot with plain boiled rice and
vegetables. *Pictured on the title page.*

YAM MAMUANG

Mango salad with monk fish　　　　　　　　　　　　　　Serves 4–6

Preparation and cooking time: 25–30 minutes + cooling and chilling

For the mango salad:

*1 large mango, peeled and
cut into julienne strips*

½ teaspoon salt

*1 tablespoon lime juice or
lemon juice*

some lettuce leaves

Yam Mamuang *means mango salad, and the version
I tasted in a food bazaar in Bangkok a few years ago
was mixed with pork. Since then, I have made mango
salad at home with different kinds of fish, and I find
monk fish is particularly good for this. When choosing
the mango, pick one that still feels rather hard.*

Put the mango strips in a bowl and sprinkle with

10–12 fresh coriander or mint leaves
For the fish:
2 tablespoons olive or groundnut oil
3 shallots or 1 onion, sliced finely
2 garlic cloves, sliced finely
2 small red chillies, de-seeded and chopped finely
5 cm (2-inch) piece of lemon grass, outer leaves discarded, chopped finely
5 cm (2-inch) piece of fresh ginger, peeled and chopped
2 tablespoons fish sauce
2 tablespoons white wine vinegar
8 tablespoons hot water
500 g (1 lb) monk fish fillets, sliced

salt and lime or lemon juice. Use the
lettuce and coriander or mint leaves to
serving dish.

Heat the oil in a large frying-pan and fry
chopped or sliced ingredients (but not the
stirring all the time, for 2 minutes. Add the fish
sauce, vinegar and water; simmer for another
2 minutes. Then add the sliced fish fillets. Let
everything simmer for 3 minutes. Remove from
the heat and cover the pan for 5 minutes. Take
off the cover and let the fish cool to room
temperature.

When the fish is cool, arrange the mangoes on
top of the lettuce leaves and the fish on top of the
mangoes. Chill for 45 minutes, and serve.

SAMBAL GORENG SOTONG

Squid in rich coconut-milk sauce   Serves 4–6

Preparation time: about 15 minutes + 20 minutes cooking

450 ml (¾ pint) hot water
5 cm (2-inch) piece of fresh lemon grass
2 kaffir lime, lemon or bay leaves
2 ripe tomatoes, peeled and chopped
125 g (4 oz) creamed coconut, chopped
1 kg (2 lb) small squid, cut into small pieces

Sambal goreng *is a generic name for dishes that are
found all over Indonesia and Malaysia;* sotong *is
squid. You can now buy squid in Britain that are
already cleaned, and quite often without the tentacles.
All you need do is cut them into small pieces and rinse
under the cold tap. They are then ready to be put into
your* sambal goreng *sauce.*

Put all the ingredients for the paste in a blender
or food processor, and blend until smooth.

Put the paste in a saucepan, bring to the boil
and stir continuously for 4 minutes. Add the
water, lemon grass and kaffir lime, lemon or bay
leaves. Bring back to the boil and let the mixture

the paste:

3 shallots or 1 small onion, chopped

2 garlic cloves

5 cm (2-inch) piece of fresh ginger, peeled and sliced

3 large red chillies, de-seeded and chopped

1 teaspoon shrimp paste (optional)

1 teaspoon ground coriander

1 teaspoon paprika

½ teaspoon salt

1 tablespoon tamarind water (page 14) or lemon juice

2 tablespoons olive or groundnut oil

2 tablespoons cold water

bubble gently for 20 minutes. Add the chopped tomatoes and creamed coconut and stir to dissolve the coconut. Simmer gently, stirring all the time, for 2 minutes. Adjust the seasoning. Up to this point the sauce can be made well in advance. It can be refrigerated for up to 24 hours, but not frozen.

Just before serving, put the sauce into a saucepan and bring it to a rolling boil. Stir, put in the squid pieces and simmer for 3 minutes only. Take out and discard the lemon grass and kaffir lime, lemon or bay leaves. Serve hot with plain boiled rice, accompanied by stir-fried vegetables or a salad.

FISH MOOLIE

Malaysian fish curry   Serves 4–6

Preparation time: 20 minutes + 40–45 minutes cooking

900 ml (1½ pints) coconut milk made from desiccated coconut (page 10)

1 kg (2 lb) fish, cleaned

For the paste:

4 shallots or 1 onion, chopped roughly

5 cm (2-inch) piece of fresh ginger, peeled and sliced

5 cm (2-inch) piece of fresh lemon grass, outer leaf discarded

5 cm (2-inch) piece of fresh galingale, peeled and chopped

If you can get red snapper or grouper from the fish counter, have the fish well cleaned, including the head. You then cook the fish whole or cut it in two. Your fish curry will look, as well as taste, authentic. But if you don't care to see a fish head on your plate, use fish steaks. You have a wide choice here: besides red snapper or grouper, you can use turbot, halibut, cod or haddock steaks.

Put all the ingredients for the paste into a blender or food processor with 6 tablespoons of the coconut milk and blend until smooth.

Pour the paste into a saucepan or wok, bring to the boil and stir continuously for 4 minutes.

Fish Moolie (Malaysian fish curry)
Sambal Goreng Sotong (Squid in rich coconut-milk sauce)

48

3 large red chillies, de-seeded and chopped roughly
3 candlenuts or 6 blanched almonds, chopped
½ teaspoon turmeric
½ teaspoon salt, plus extra to taste

Add the remaining coconut milk. Bring to the boil again, stir, and simmer for 30 minutes, stirring often, until the quantity is reduced by half. Put in the fish and simmer for 10–15 minutes, stirring occasionally. Adjust the seasoning. Transfer into a serving dish and sprinkle with Goreng Bawang (Crispy fried shallots, page 78). Serve immediately, accompanied by plain cooked rice and vegetables of your choice or a salad.

YAM PLA MUEK

Squid salad   Serves 4–6

Preparation and cooking time: about 20 minutes + cooling and chilling

8 tablespoons groundnut oil
1 kg (2 lb) small squid, washed and cut into 1 × 2.5 cm (½-inch × 1-inch) pieces
For the dressing:
2 small red chillies, de-seeded and chopped finely
5 cm (2-inch) piece of lemon grass, outer leaves discarded, chopped finely
2 fresh kaffir lime leaves or lemon leaves, shredded finely
2 tablespoons fish sauce
2 tablespoons lemon juice
1 tablespoon mild vinegar
1 teaspoon caster sugar
For the garnish:
10 fresh mint leaves
10 fresh coriander leaves
a small cucumber, cut into 2 lengthways and sliced thinly

For this (and for the other yam *or Thai salad in this fish section), the squid, prawns or other fish can be either poached or fried. I find squid are always tender if they are fried in very hot oil for just 3 minutes. However, they do spit quite a lot, and you may prefer to poach them gently, also for just 3 minutes. If you overrun the time, you need to continue poaching them for 40 minutes or longer to get them tender again.*

Heat the oil in a wok or a deep frying-pan, and fry the squid in 3 batches for 3 minutes only each time. Drain in a colander.

Mix the dressing well, and dress the squid in a glass bowl while they are still warm. Leave them to cool, then chill for at least 30 minutes. Add the garnish and stir gently so the leaves and cucumber are well coated. Serve cold, as a first course.

MEAT AND POULTRY

At home, we usually cut the meat into quite
small pieces, and cook it with vegetables and
potatoes, though we still eat it with a lot of rice.
Many people keep their own chickens and
ducks, which of course are free-range, lead very
energetic lives and are consequently rather
tougher than the ones you buy in Britain.

LAAB

A spicy beef salad   Serves 4

Preparation and cooking time: 30 minutes + cooling

3 tablespoons Thai fragrant
rice

3 tablespoons groundnut oil

500 g (1 lb) good lean beef,
such as rump steak or
topside, minced

3 shallots, chopped finely

3 garlic cloves, chopped
finely

3 small red chillies, de-
seeded and chopped finely

a large pinch of chilli
powder

3 tablespoons lime or lemon
juice

2 tablespoons fish sauce

2 tablespoons finely
chopped fresh coriander
leaves

2 tablespoons chopped fresh
flat-leaf parsley

salt if necessary

12 crisp lettuce or chicory
leaves

*This is a northern Thai dish. Made with minced beef,
with roasted ground rice added to give a nice nutty
taste, it is normally eaten wrapped in crisp lettuce
leaves, or you can serve it as a first course piled on
lettuce or chicory leaves.*

*For the roasted rice, use Thai fragrant rice, also
called 'jasmine rice'.*

Put the rice in a heavy-bottomed frying-pan,
and roast, stirring with a wooden spoon, until
the rice is a good yellow colour. Let it cool, and
grind it in a coffee-grinder until you get a fairly
coarse ground rice flour.

Heat the oil in a wok or large frying-pan and
fry the minced beef in it, stirring all the time, for
4 minutes. Add the rest of the ingredients except
the rice flour, coriander, parsley and salad
leaves. Stir again on a fairly high heat for 2 more
minutes, then add the rice flour and herbs.
Adjust the seasoning. Leave the dish to cool.
Serve it cold as a starter, piled up on the leaves.

MASAMAN

A Thai beef curry   Serves 4–6

Preparation time: 30 minutes + about 2 hours cooking

1.2 litres (2 pints) coconut
milk (page 10), made from
250 g (8 oz) desiccated
coconut

---

1 kg (2 lb) brisket or
silverside, cut into 2.5 cm
(1-inch) cubes *

---

1 teaspoon demerara sugar

---

3 kaffir lime leaves

---

1 teaspoon salt, plus extra if
necessary

---

1 small pineapple, peeled
and chopped (optional)

To be roasted:

---

4 small dried chillies

---

3 shallots or 1 small onion,
unpeeled

---

3 garlic cloves, unpeeled

2.5 cm (1-inch) piece of
lemon grass, outer leaves
discarded

---

2 tablespoons chopped
coriander root and stalk

---

1 tablespoon coriander seeds

---

1 teaspoon cumin seeds

---

2 green cardamoms

---

2 cloves

**To be added before
blending:**

---

2 tablespoons groundnut or
olive oil

---

2 tablespoons tamarind
water (page 14) or lemon
juice

Quite a lot of Eastern dishes are just as good after reheating as they are when freshly cooked. Masaman is one of them, and it also freezes well. You can leave it in the freezer for up to 3 months, but make sure you thaw it out completely before you reheat it. Reheating takes 30 minutes (not more) in a medium-hot oven or in a saucepan on a low heat. The advantage of the saucepan is that you can stir the Masaman often. The sauce for this curry should be dark brown and very thick. The rich brown colour comes partly from the spices, most of which are dry-roasted before being made into a paste.

Put all the ingredients for roasting on a baking tray and roast in the oven at Gas Mark 4/180°C/350°F for about 10 minutes. Alternatively, put them in a heavy frying-pan and brown them on the stove, stirring them with a wooden spoon frequently. Peel the shallots or onion and garlic and transfer the whole lot to a blender or food processor. Add all the other ingredients for blending, with 3 tablespoons of the coconut milk and blend until you have a smooth paste.

Put this curry paste in a large saucepan. Bring to the boil and stir continuously for 4–5 minutes. Add the meat, and stir until all the cubes are coated with the paste. Cover the pan for 3 minutes only; uncover and stir, and add the remaining coconut milk, demerara sugar, kaffir lime leaves and salt to taste.

Bring this to the boil, turn down the heat a little and let the curry bubble, uncovered, for 1½ hours. By this time the sauce will have thickened quite a lot. Adjust the seasoning, add the pineapple, if used, and continue cooking, stirring all the time, for 10–15 minutes.

*Gaeng Keo Wan Kai (A green curry of chicken)
Masaman (A Thai beef curry)*

52

½ tablespoon ground
galingale

½ teaspoon grated nutmeg

½ teaspoon ground
cinnamon

2 teaspoons crumbled
shrimp paste

Alternatively, after adjusting the seasoning
you can put the curry in an ovenproof container,
cover it with aluminium foil and finish the
cooking in the oven at Gas Mark ½/120°C/
250°F for at least 30 minutes or up to 1 hour.
Serve hot with plenty of plain boiled rice
accompanied by cooked vegetables or salad.

GAENG KEO WAN KAI

A green curry of chicken   Serves 4–6

Preparation time: 30 minutes + 50–55 minutes cooking

1 kg (2 lb) chicken breast
and thigh meat, cut into 2.5
cm (1-inch) pieces

1.2 litres (2 pints) coconut
milk, made from 175 g (6
oz) desiccated coconut

500 g (1 lb) small new
potatoes, scrubbed

For the paste:

4 shallots or 1 medium-size
onion, chopped

3 garlic cloves, chopped

10 cm (4-inch) piece of
lemon grass, outer leaves
discarded, chopped

2.5 cm (1-inch) piece of
fresh galingale, peeled and
chopped

2 kaffir lime leaves,
shredded

1 teaspoon ground pepper

1 tablespoon roasted
coriander seeds

1 tablespoon roasted cumin
seeds

½ teaspoon grated nutmeg

5 fresh green chillies,
de-seeded and chopped

*The sauce for this Thai curry can be very liquid and
runny, or it can be reduced and made quite thick.
I myself like it not too thick, and I like to have some
new potatoes cooking in it. The sauce is made from
curry paste mixed with coconut milk.*

Put all the ingredients for the paste in a blender
or food processor with 3 tablespoons of the
coconut milk, and blend until smooth. Transfer
this paste into a saucepan, bring to the boil, then
stir all the time for 3–4 minutes. Add the chicken
pieces and stir until all the pieces are well coated
with the paste. Turn down the heat, cover the
pan and let it simmer for 4 minutes. Uncover,
stir again and add the remaining coconut milk.
Simmer, stirring frequently, for 40 minutes.

Add the new potatoes, and continue cooking
for 10–15 minutes or until the potatoes are done.
Serve hot with plain boiled rice.

1 green pepper (optional),
de-seeded and chopped

1 teaspoon chopped
coriander roots or stalks
(optional)

2 tablespoons chopped fresh
coriander leaves

1 tablespoon fish sauce

1 teaspoon salt

2 tablespoons tamarind
water (page 14) or lemon
juice

2 tablespoons olive oil

BABI KECAP

Pork in soy sauce with mushrooms   Serves 4

Preparation and cooking time: 40 minutes + marinating

1 kg (2 lb) fillet or leg of
pork, cut into small cubes

450 ml (¾ pint) vegetable
oil

250 g (8 oz) button
mushrooms, quartered or
halved

3 garlic cloves, chopped
finely

5 cm (2-inch) piece of fresh
ginger, peeled and chopped
finely

3 tablespoons hot water

2 tablespoons dark soy sauce

4 spring onions, sliced
thinly

2 tablespoons chopped flat-
leaf parsley

¼ teaspoon ground white
pepper

2 tablespoons rice wine or
dry sherry (optional)

*If you are not sure that all your guests or children will
like Indonesian food, start them off with this recipe,
because I think everybody likes soy sauce. Also, this
dish is not chilli-hot and the only other exotic
ingredient is ginger. Although we usually eat this
pork dish with rice, it is equally good eaten with
potatoes or pasta.*

Put the pork cubes in a bowl and mix in all the
ingredients for the marinade. Leave to marinate
for 30 minutes.

Heat the oil in a wok or frying-pan, and fry
the mushrooms in 2 batches for 3 minutes each
time. Take them out with a slotted spoon and
put them on a plate lined with some absorbent
paper. In the remaining oil fry the pork pieces in
3 batches, each time for 3 minutes. Take them
out with a slotted spoon and drain in a colander.

You may need to add just another tablespoon
of oil to the wok or pan. Heat the oil again, then
fry the chopped garlic and ginger, stirring all the
time, for 2 minutes. Add the hot water and soy
sauce, stir and add the fried meat and
mushrooms. Stir them around for 1 minute,

For the marinade:

1 tablespoon light soy sauce

1 teaspoon mild vinegar

2 teaspoons plain flour

a large pinch of ground white pepper

1 garlic clove, crushed

then add the rest of the ingredients. Stir, and keep stirring for 1 more minute. Taste, and adjust the seasoning. Serve immediately, with plain boiled rice, fried rice, potatoes or pasta, accompanied by a salad. *Pictured on page 4.*

BEBEK BETUTU

Traditional Balinese duck   Serves 6

Preparation time: 40 minutes + marinating + 3–4 hours cooking

175 g (6 oz) curly kale or vine leaves or young courgette leaves or spinach, blanched, squeezed dry and shredded

1.5–1.75 kg (3½–4 lb) oven-ready duckling

For the paste:

4 shallots or 1 onion, chopped

3 garlic cloves, chopped

3 red chillies, de-seeded and chopped, or 1 teaspoon chilli powder

2 candlenuts or 5 tablespoons very thick coconut milk (page 10)

2 teaspoons coriander seeds

1 teaspoon cumin seeds

2 cloves

½ teaspoon ground cinnamon

¼ teaspoon ground or grated nutmeg

½ teaspoon ground turmeric

When I last visited Bali, the monks of Ubud still cooked this traditional Balinese dish in the old-fashioned way, leaving it for six or seven hours in the embers of a fire laid in a shallow trench. The duck is stuffed and wrapped in seludang mayang, *the flower-sheath of a particular kind of palm, then in layers and layers of banana leaves. The alternative is to use aluminium foil as described here, and cook it in the oven for 3–4 hours. The leaves for the stuffing ought to be young cassava leaves, but these are still unavailable in Britain. So I use curly kale in the autumn and winter; in spring and summer I use very young vine or courgette leaves. Alternatively, I use spinach, which is available all the year round.*

Put all the ingredients for the paste in a blender or food processor, and blend them until smooth. Transfer the paste into a wok or a saucepan, heat and bring it to the boil, then stir all the time for 4–5 minutes or until the smell of raw shallots and garlic has been replaced by a pleasant spicy fragrance. Leave to cool.

When the paste is cool, mix half of it in a bowl with the shredded leaves. Then rub the remaining paste on the duckling, inside as well as outside. Stuff the shredded leaves into the duckling. Wrap the stuffed duckling loosely in 3

Bebek Betutu (Traditional Balinese duck)

¼ teaspoon ground galingale	or 4 layers of aluminium foil. Everything up to this point can be done the day before, and the parcel can be left in the fridge overnight so that the duckling marinates thoroughly.
½ teaspoon white pepper	
5 cm (2-inch) piece of lemon grass, outer leaves discarded	
2.5 cm (1-inch) piece of shrimp paste (optional)	
1 teaspoon salt	
2 tablespoons lime or lemon juice	
3 tablespoons olive oil	
2 tablespoons water	

¼ teaspoon ground galingale

½ teaspoon white pepper

5 cm (2-inch) piece of lemon grass, outer leaves discarded

2.5 cm (1-inch) piece of shrimp paste (optional)

1 teaspoon salt

2 tablespoons lime or lemon juice

3 tablespoons olive oil

2 tablespoons water

or 4 layers of aluminium foil. Everything up to this point can be done the day before, and the parcel can be left in the fridge overnight so that the duckling marinates thoroughly.

To cook, preheat the oven to Gas Mark 4/ 180°C/350°F and then put in the parcel. Cook for 3–4 hours, turning down the oven to Gas Mark ½/120°C/250°F after the first hour.

To serve, unwrap the parcel and put the duckling onto a large dish. Separate and discard the oil from the cooking juices. Put the cooking juices in a small saucepan, add to this all the stuffing, which has now become a dark coloured purée (but tastes delicious), heat, and serve it as a thick sauce. The duckling will be so tender that the meat will come off the bones very easily. Pile the meat on a warm serving dish and pour the sauce over it. Serve with plenty of plain cooked rice.

RENDANG

A traditional West Sumatran beef dish   Serves 8–10

Preparation time: 30 minutes + 3 hours cooking

1.8 litres (3 pints) coconut milk, made from 2 coconuts or 750 g (1½ lb) desiccated coconut (page 10)

1.5 kg (3 lb) brisket, or silverside, cut into 2 cm (¾-inch) cubes

1 stem of fresh lemon grass, halved and bruised

2 kaffir lime leaves or 1 bay leaf

1½ teaspoons salt, plus extra to taste

For the paste:

6 shallots or 2 onions, chopped

4 garlic cloves, chopped

A well-cooked Rendang is brown, sometimes almost black. It should be chunky and dry, yet succulent, with the dryness of meat that has absorbed its juices and its sauce during a long period of cooking. This is the only dish that I know of that passes from boiling to frying without any interruption. The cooking time is therefore very long.

Put all the ingredients for the paste in a blender or food processor with 4 tablespoons of the coconut milk. Blend until smooth.

Put the remaining coconut milk in a wok or a large saucepan. Add the meat, which must be completely covered by the coconut milk, and the paste from the blender and the rest of the ingredients, stir, and start cooking on a medium heat, uncovered. Let this simmer for 2 hours, stirring from time to time. By this time the coconut milk will have become oily, and the

5 cm (2-inch) piece of fresh ginger, peeled and chopped

1 teaspoon ground turmeric

6 red chillies, de-seeded and chopped, or 2 teaspoons chilli powder

½ teaspoon ground galingale

dish now needs to be stirred frequently. Taste and add more salt if necessary, and cook for a further 30 minutes. When it becomes thick and brown, stir all the time for about 15 minutes, until the oil has almost disappeared, absorbed by the meat. Now the dish is ready. Serve hot with plenty of rice.

OPOR AYAM

Chicken in white coconut sauce   Serves 4

Preparation time: 15 minutes + 1 hour 50 minutes cooking

1 medium-size chicken

600 ml (1 pint) coconut milk made from 150 g (5 oz) desiccated coconut (page 10)

8 tablespoons natural or Greek yogurt

For the paste:

3 shallots or 1 medium-size white onion, chopped

5 garlic cloves, chopped

2 teaspoons ground coriander

1 teaspoon ground white pepper

a large pinch of ground cumin

2 kaffir lime leaves

4 candlenuts or 6 blanched almonds

½ teaspoon shrimp paste (optional)

1 teaspoon salt

This is my most recent version of Opor Ayam, after experimenting with quite a lot of alternatives to the original ingredients. Opor needs to have a white sauce, and I find that a combination of coconut milk and natural unsweetened yogurt, or better still the creamy Greek yogurt, gives you just the right creamy-sour taste. Another difference between this and the original Opor Ayam is that I roast the chicken first, before cutting it into serving pieces and cooking it in the coconut and yogurt sauce.

Roast the chicken for 50 minutes in an oven preheated to Gas Mark 4/180°C/350°F. When it is done, take it out of the oven and let it cool while you prepare the sauce.

Put all the ingredients for the paste in a blender or food processor with 4 tablespoons of coconut milk and blend until smooth. Put this paste into a large saucepan, heat and bring it to the boil. Stir it continuously for 4–5 minutes, then add the remaining coconut milk. Bring it back to the boil and simmer for 30 minutes, stirring often.

By now the chicken should be cool enough to handle. Joint it into 8 pieces, and remove some of the bones, such as the neck bone and the ribs. Bring the coconut milk to a rolling boil and add the chicken pieces; continue to cook on a medium heat for 20 minutes. Add the yogurt, a spoonful at a time, while continuing to stir the contents of the saucepan. Simmer for another 10 minutes. Adjust the seasoning and serve hot with plain boiled rice or boiled new potatoes accompanied by a cooked vegetable or a salad.

CHIANG RAI

Spicy minced pork   Serves 4

Preparation and cooking time: 25 minutes

500 g (1 lb) minced pork

2 teaspoons whole green peppercorns

3 kaffir lime leaves, shredded finely

2 tablespoons fish sauce

1 teaspoon brown sugar

10–15 fresh basil leaves

salt and pepper

1 large red chilli, de-seeded and cut into tiny strips, to garnish

For the paste:

5 garlic cloves, chopped

4 large red chillies, de-seeded and chopped

2 teaspoons finely chopped coriander root

3 tablespoons groundnut oil

1 tablespoon hot water

Chiang Rai is a town in the northern part of Thailand, so it was never the name of a dish or recipe in any other Thai cookery book. This recipe was given to me by the Blue Elephant restaurant in Fulham Broadway, London. The first time I tried it there I thought it tasted very good; when I asked why it was called Chiang Rai, the assistant manager, Kun Manat, told me that whenever he goes home to Thailand he eats at a restaurant in Chiang Rai, and this is his favourite dish.

Put all the ingredients for the paste in a blender and blend until smooth. Transfer this paste into a wok or a frying-pan. Heat and stir continuously for 4 minutes. Increase the heat and add the minced pork and stir all the time for 3 minutes. Add the rest of the ingredients except the basil leaves and chilli strips, and continue stirring for 3 more minutes or until the meat is almost dry. Put in the basil leaves and give just one more stir around. Adjust the seasoning. Garnish with chilli strips. Serve hot with rice or a salad.

*Opor Ayam (Chicken in white coconut sauce)
Chiang Rai (Spicy minced pork)*

GULÉ KAMBING

Preparation time: 25 minutes + 65 minutes cooking

900 ml (1½ pints) coconut milk, made from 175 g (6 oz) desiccated coconut

1 kg (2 lb) lamb leg or shoulder, cut into small cubes

5 cm (2-inch) piece of lemon grass, washed

2 kaffir lime leaves or 1 bay leaf

½ teaspoon brown sugar

300 ml (½-pint) hot water

For the paste:

4 shallots or 1 onion, chopped

2 garlic cloves, chopped

2.5 cm (1-inch) piece of fresh ginger, peeled and chopped

4 candlenuts or 6 blanched almonds

1 teaspoon ground coriander

½ teaspoon ground cinnamon

1 teaspoon chilli powder

¼ teaspoon ground galingale

½ teaspoon ground turmeric

2 cloves

¼ teaspoon ground white pepper

1 kaffir lime or bay leaf

3 tablespoons tamarind water (page 14)

1 teaspoon salt, plus extra if necessary

This is a liquid lamb stew – or you can think of it as a very meaty soup. Do not use flour to thicken the sauce; if you want it thicker, use very thick coconut milk (page 10) or less water.

Put all the ingredients for the paste in a blender or food processor with 4 tablespoons of coconut milk, and blend until smooth. Transfer this paste into a large saucepan, heat and bring it to the boil, then stir continuously for 4–5 minutes. Add the meat cubes, and stir these until all the cubes are well coated with the paste and the meat has changed colour. Add the lemon grass, kaffir lime or bay leaves, sugar and hot water, stir and cover the saucepan. Simmer for 20 minutes.

Remove the saucepan lid and add the coconut milk. Bring the contents back to the boil and simmer for 45 minutes, stirring often. Taste, and add more salt if necessary. Take out the lemon grass and the kaffir lime or bay leaves before serving the stew hot with plain boiled rice. The best way to eat *gulé* is to put some boiled rice in a soup-plate, ladle the *gulé* over it, and eat it with a spoon.

BEBEK ASAM PEDAS

Duck in hot and sour sauce   Serves 4

Preparation and cooking time: 35–40 minutes

4 duck breasts with the skin, cut into thin slices diagonally

1 teaspoon salt, plus extra to taste

125 ml (4 fl oz) vegetable oil

227 g (8 oz) can of bamboo shoots, rinsed and sliced finely

For the paste:

4 shallots or 1 medium-size onion, chopped

2 garlic cloves, chopped

2.5 cm (1-inch) piece of fresh ginger, peeled and chopped

1 teaspoon ground coriander

3 large red chillies, de-seeded and chopped, or 1 teaspoon chilli powder

1/2 teaspoon ground turmeric

4 candlenuts or 6 blanched almonds, chopped

2 tablespoons tamarind water (page 14), or mild vinegar

2 tablespoons hot water

Most Malaysians and Indonesians prefer a hot-and-sour sauce to the Chinese sweet-and-sour. This sauce is very red, really hot and sour, and delicious. It is usually made with tamarind and lots of red chillies crushed into a smooth paste. The recipe that follows will look and taste just as good but will not be burning hot. If tamarind is not available, you can use mild vinegar instead.

Put the duck slices in a bowl and rub well with the salt. Chill for 20 minutes.

Meanwhile, put all the ingredients for the paste in a blender or food processor and blend until smooth.

In a wok or large saucepan, heat the oil and fry the duck slices in batches for 3 minutes each time. Take out with a slotted spoon and put on absorbent paper to drain. Discard the remaining oil, except for about 2 tablespoonfuls; in this, fry the paste from the blender, stirring continuously, for 5 minutes. Add the meat and keep on stirring for 2 minutes. Then add the bamboo shoots and stir for 2 minutes longer. Taste, and add salt if necessary. Serve hot with rice or pasta.

63

VEGETABLES

The vegetable dishes in this section are intended as accompaniments to the main course, though most of them are quite suitable for a one-dish meal at lunch or supper time. Recipes like Gado-Gado (page 72), for example, and those using tofu and coconut, are quite filling and full of protein, so I recommend them highly to vegetarians who want something different and a little more spicy than usual. If for any reason you don't want to use shrimp paste, fish sauce or oyster sauce, these can be omitted, or – if you feel the need for a substitute – soy sauce can be used instead.

TUMIS PEDAS KACANG PANJANG

Spiced braised yard-long beans   Serves 4

Preparation and cooking time: 30 minutes

500 g (1 lb) yard-long or french beans, cut into 2.5 cm (1-inch) pieces

125 ml (4 fl oz) hot water

For the paste:

4 shallots or 1 medium-size onion, chopped

2 garlic cloves, chopped

2.5 cm (1-inch) piece of fresh ginger, peeled and chopped

1 tablespoon yellow bean sauce or 1 teaspoon shrimp paste (optional)

3 small dried red chillies, or ½ teaspoon chilli powder

1 tablespoon tamarind water (page 14) or lemon juice

2 tablespoons groundnut or olive oil

Although yard-long beans taste quite different from young french beans, I often use french beans for this dish, which is then called Tumis pedas buncis.

Put all the ingredients for the paste in a blender or food processor and blend them until smooth. Transfer this paste into a wok or a large frying-pan, bring it to the boil and stir most of the time for 3–4 minutes. Increase the heat and add the beans. Stir and turn the beans for 1 minute, add the hot water, stir once, then cover the wok or pan. Leave it to simmer for 2 minutes. Uncover, and stir it again for another minute. Adjust the seasoning and serve hot as a side vegetable dish to accompany a main course.

URAP

Raw vegetables in spiced coconut dressing   Serves 4–6

Preparation time: 25–30 minutes

4 medium-size carrots, peeled and grated

125 g (4 oz) bean sprouts, washed and drained

125 g (4 oz) watercress, cleaned and chopped roughly

125 g (4 oz) mangetout, sliced thinly diagonally

125 g (4 oz) white cabbage, shredded finely

For the coconut dressing:

1 coconut, shelled, brown inner skin peeled away

1 teaspoon fried shrimp paste, or 1 teaspoon anchovy paste

2 garlic cloves, crushed

juice of 1 lime

½ teaspoon chilli powder

½ teaspoon soft brown sugar (optional)

1 teaspoon salt

For this salad you can use exactly the same vegetables as for Gado-Gado (page 72), and instead of peanut sauce use the coconut dressing described here. However, many Indonesians, especially those who live in West Java, like their Urap made from uncooked vegetables. So here is my suggestion for a good combination of them.

Grate the coconut with a hand grater, or put the broken fragments of it into your food processor and process it until you get fine coconut crumbs. Put the fried shrimp paste (or anchovy paste) on a plate and mash it with the back of a spoon. Add the crushed garlic, lime juice, chilli powder, sugar (if used) and salt. Mix well. Then add this paste mixture to the grated coconut. Mix well again, taste and add more salt if necessary.

To serve, put all the prepared vegetables into a salad bowl, and mix in the coconut dressing. Serve as a side dish to accompany the main course, or by itself as a first course; or as a snack lunch it serves four people.

ASINAN TAHU DAN TAUGE

A tofu and bean sprout salad   Serves 4–6

Preparation time: 15–20 minutes

For the dressing:

2 green chillies, de-seeded and sliced thinly

2 shallots or 1 small onion, sliced finely

In Indonesia, one meaning of asinan *is a salad with hot and sour dressing – a clear dressing made of vinegar, seasoned with chilli, salt and sugar, without oil. This dressing is used mainly for raw vegetables and fruit that have been cut into very fine julienne strips. Such a salad is a good accompaniment to a spicy*

2 garlic cloves, sliced finely

6 tablespoons white distilled vinegar

2 teaspoons granulated sugar

1 teaspoon salt

6 tablespoons hot water

Other ingredients:

1 large, crisp, eating apple, cut into julienne strips

200 g (7 oz) tofu, cubed

4 spring onions, cleaned and sliced thinly

125 g (4 oz) carrots, grated coarsely or cut into julienne

125 g (4 oz) bean sprouts, washed

hot meat dish. But here, I am making this asinan *for vegetarians and vegans, adding tofu to make it suitable for a one-dish cold meal. Tofu and bean sprouts are a classic combination, but here I am adding other ingredients as well.*

First, mix all the dressing ingredients in a glass bowl. Put in the apple at once, to prevent discolouration. Then add the rest of the ingredients. Mix well, and keep in a cool place or in the fridge until needed. You can prepare this salad several hours in advance; take it out of the fridge at least 30 minutes before serving. Serve at room temperature, as a light lunch or accompaniment to the main course.

URAP PANGGANG SAYUR

Baked courgettes with spiced coconut   Serves 4–6

Preparation time: 15 minutes + 15 minutes cooking

3 tablespoons groundnut or olive oil

1 onion, sliced finely

4 garlic cloves, sliced finely

3 large red chillies, de-seeded and sliced thinly diagonally, or ½ teaspoon chilli powder

1 teaspoon ground coriander

1 teaspoon shrimp paste (optional)

6–8 tablespoons desiccated coconut

300 ml (½ pint) water

1 tablespoon tomato purée

1 teaspoon salt

I was really quite surprised when, as far back as 1964, just a few months after I first came to London and was giving my very first dinner party, this dish was approved enthusiastically by my English guests. On that occasion, I made it with cauliflower – yet it is only recently, hundreds of dinner parties later, that I realise this dish is similar to European vegetable dishes au gratin. The only exotic part of it is the coconut, which is used as you would use grated cheese or breadcrumbs.

Preheat the oven to Gas Mark 4/180°C/350°F. Heat the oil in a wok or a large shallow saucepan, and fry the onion, garlic, chillies and coriander, stirring continuously, for 2 minutes. Add the rest of the ingredients, except the courgettes. Let this simmer for 3 minutes, stirring occasionally.

At the end of this time almost all the water will have been absorbed by the desiccated coconut. Reserve about 4 tablespoonfuls of this coconut

. 750 g (1½ lbs) courgettes,
sliced thinly

mixture. Add the courgettes to the remainder,
stir and turn them around for 1–2 minutes so
that they are all well coated. Transfer the whole
lot to an ovenproof or gratin dish, level off the
top with a fork, and spread the reserved coconut
evenly over it. Then bake, uncovered, for 15
minutes. Serve hot with a main course.

PAT PAK RUAM MITR

Stir-fried mixed green vegetables   Serves 4–6

Preparation and cooking time: 30 minutes

175 g (6 oz) water spinach
or watercress

2–3 teaspoons groundnut or
olive oil

4 garlic cloves, sliced very
finely

2.5 cm (1-inch) piece of
fresh ginger, peeled and
sliced finely

175 g (6 oz) broccoli florets

125 g (4 oz) mangetout,
topped and tailed

2 medium-size green
peppers, de-seeded and cut
into 8

2 teaspoons whole green
peppercorns, or ¼ teaspoon
freshly ground black pepper

1 tablespoon fish sauce

1 tablespoon oyster sauce

½ tablespoon sugar
(optional)

4 spring onions, cut into 2
cm (¾-inch) lengths

salt to taste, if necessary

*For this Thai version of a stir-fried vegetable dish I
have chosen a combination of vegetables that are very
quick to cook; they should come to the table crisp,
crunchy and green.*

Trim and discard the hard lower stalks of the
water spinach or watercress. Wash the leaves,
then drain them in a colander.

Heat the oil in a wok or a large shallow
saucepan. Fry the garlic and ginger, stirring all
the time, for 1 minute. Add the broccoli florets,
stir them around for 2 minutes, then add the
mangetout and green peppers. Stir and turn all
the vegetables again, on a very high heat, for
2 minutes. Now add the rest of the ingredients
and continue to cook, stirring often, for another
2 minutes. Adjust the seasoning, adding a little
salt if necessary. Transfer to a warm serving dish
and serve immediately. *Pictured on page 5.*

SAYUR MASAK LEMAK

Cauliflower and potatoes with creamed coconut   Serves 4–6

Preparation and cooking time: 20 minutes

375 g (12 oz) small waxy potatoes, or new potatoes, scrubbed and quartered

1 small cauliflower, cut into florets

50 g (2 oz) creamed coconut, chopped

6 tablespoons water

3 garlic cloves, sliced finely (optional)

2 kaffir lime leaves or 1 bay leaf

1 tablespoon chopped fresh chives

salt to taste

For the paste:

3 shallots or 1 small onion, chopped

3 candlenuts or 5 blanched almonds, chopped

1 teaspoon ground coriander

½ teaspoon ground cumin

½ teaspoon ground white pepper

½ teaspoon ground turmeric

½ teaspoon salt

2 tablespoons water

2 tablespoons groundnut or olive oil

Masak Lemak *in Malaysia almost invariably means 'cooked with* lemak*', or, literally, fat; but here it means 'cooked in coconut cream or coconut milk'. Usually this dish is made with a lot of sauce, maybe reduced slightly by longer cooking. Here I do not reduce the sauce, but actually make it thick to coat the vegetables.*

Boil the potatoes in slightly salted water for 12–15 minutes or until cooked. Boil the cauliflower for 2 minutes, drain it in a colander and refresh under cold running water. Make the paste while you are boiling the potatoes.

Put all the ingredients for the paste in a blender or food processor and blend them until smooth. Transfer the paste to a bowl. You can prepare everything up to this point well in advance.

When you are ready to cook, put the paste from the bowl into a wok or a large, shallow saucepan. Bring this to the boil, and cook for 4 minutes, stirring most of the time to prevent it from burning and sticking to the bottom of the wok or pan. Add the creamed coconut and the water, garlic (if used), and kaffir lime leaves or bay leaf. Bring this back to the boil, stir for a few seconds and then add the potatoes and cauliflower. Stir and turn them for 1–2 minutes, or until the vegetables become hot. Add the chives and adjust the seasoning. Stir for a few more seconds, then discard the kaffir lime or bay leaf and transfer the vegetables and the thick sauce into a warm serving dish. Serve hot as an accompaniment to a meat or fish main course.

Tumis Pedas Kacang Panjang (Spiced braised yard-long beans)
Sayur Masak Lemak (Cauliflower and potatoes with creamed coconut)

TUMIS BENDI

Preparation and cooking time: 20 minutes

2 tablespoons vegetable oil

1 onion, chopped finely

4 garlic cloves, chopped finely

3 large green chillies, de-seeded and sliced thinly diagonally

1 teaspoon ground coriander

½ teaspoon ground cumin

2 ripe tomatoes, skinned, de-seeded and chopped roughly

425 g (14 oz) young okra, washed, trimmed and patted dry

½ teaspoon sugar

½ teaspoon salt

2 tablespoons chopped fresh coriander or flat-leaf parsley

Okra or 'ladies' fingers' have been available for a long time in Britain, but are still considered an acquired taste, perhaps because they have a rather slimy texture. They are more often used in Indian cooking, but the Malaysians use them quite a lot as well. Choose young ones, which are smaller in size, and to prepare them simply trim off a little bit of the bottom part, which is rather hard.

Heat the oil in a wok or frying-pan, and fry the onion, garlic and green chillies, stirring them continuously, for 2 minutes. Add the coriander and cumin, stir again and add the chopped tomatoes and okra. Stir; then cover the wok or pan and simmer for 4 minutes. Remove the cover, and add the sugar and salt. Stir again for 1 minute. Adjust the seasoning, and add the coriander or parsley. Stir for 30 seconds.
Transfer into a warm serving dish and serve hot as an accompaniment to the main course. Okra will go well with lamb or beef dishes.

ACAR KUNING

Mixed cooked vegetables in piquant sauce   Serves 4–6

Preparation and cooking time: 30–35 minutes

125 ml (4 fl oz) water

8–10 small pickling onions, peeled (optional)

175 g (6 oz) french beans, topped and tailed and cut into 2 or 3 pieces

175 g (6 oz) carrots, peeled and cut into sticks about the same length as the beans

175 g (6 oz) cauliflower florets

1 teaspoon mustard powder

1 teaspoon sugar

1 tablespoon white distilled vinegar

8–10 small red or green chillies (optional)

salt and pepper to taste

For the paste:

2 shallots or ½ onion, chopped

2 garlic cloves, chopped

3 candlenuts or 5 blanched almonds, chopped

1 large red or green chilli, de-seeded and chopped

½ teaspoon ground turmeric

2 tablespoons white distilled vinegar

2 tablespoons groundnut or olive oil

½ teaspoon salt

Acar *(pronounced 'achar') is a generic term in many Eastern countries for a vegetable or mixed-vegetable dish, raw or cooked, lightly pickled with vinegar, and mildly or very hotly spiced.* Kuning *means yellow, so here we use turmeric to get the right colour. Acar is normally eaten cold, but this version can be served hot as a side dish of hot vegetables. For serving cold, on the other hand, it can be made several days ahead and kept in the fridge in a bowl covered tightly with cling film. It is also suitable for freezing. Thaw it out completely before serving.*

Put all the ingredients for the paste in a blender or food processor and blend until smooth. Transfer this paste to a wok or a large shallow saucepan. Bring to the boil, stirring most of the time, for 4 minutes. Add the water and bring this back to the boil. When it is boiling add the pickling onions (if used), stir, and cover the wok or pan for 2 minutes. Uncover and add the beans and carrots, put the cover on again and simmer for 3 minutes. Once more uncover the wok or pan, and add the cauliflower and the rest of the ingredients. Stir them around and put the cover back, and continue cooking for 3–5 more minutes. Uncover the wok or pan for the last time, adjust the seasoning and turn the vegetables over again for a few seconds. Transfer to a warm serving dish, if it is to be served hot as an accompaniment to your main course; otherwise refrigerate, to be served cold a few hours or a few days later. *Pictured on page 4.*

GADO-GADO

Mixed cooked vegetable salad in peanut sauce　　　　　　　Serves 4–6

Preparation and cooking time: 30–40 minutes

The vegetables:

125 g (4 oz) cabbage or
spring greens, shredded

125 g (4 oz) french beans,
cut into 1 cm (½-inch)
lengths

125 g (4 oz) carrots, peeled
and sliced thinly

125 g (4 oz) cauliflower
florets

125 g (4 oz) bean sprouts,
washed

For the garnish:

some lettuce leaves and
watercress

1–2 hard-boiled eggs,
quartered

1 medium-size potato,
boiled in its skin, then
peeled and sliced

¼ cucumber, sliced thinly

300 ml (¼ pint) Sambal
Kacang (A peanut sauce,
page 76)

1 tablespoon Goreng
Bawang (Crispy fried
shallots, page 78)

Indonesians love salads made from lightly-cooked vegetables with a nutty savoury sauce on top. This is one of the most popular, and is found not only in Java but in many of the other islands. The Malaysians also claim it as their national dish. We normally eat it as a lunch dish by itself, and this way it will serve four people; it can also be served as a vegetable dish to accompany a meat or fish main course with rice.

Boil the vegetables separately in slightly salted water for 3–4 minutes, except the bean sprouts which only need 2 minutes. Drain each kind separately in a colander.

To serve, arrange the lettuce leaves and watercress around the edge of a serving dish. Then pile the vegetables in the middle of the dish. Arrange the eggs, sliced potatoes and sliced cucumber on top.

Heat the peanut sauce in a small saucepan until hot; add more water if it is too thick. Adjust the seasoning, and pour the sauce over the vegetables. Sprinkle the fried shallots on top. Serve warm or cold.

Gado-Gado (Mixed cooked vegetable salad in peanut sauce)

SAUCES, SAMBALS AND RELISHES

This is just a small selection of the hot and spicy accompaniments that add piquancy and kick to the already spicy, aromatic dishes of Thailand, Indonesia and Malaysia. If you wonder why we still need these enhancements to our cooking, I must mention here that, for everyday eating, quite a lot of people in these three countries either prefer, or can only afford, simple food.

Most *sambals* take a lot of time and trouble to prepare. So most of these relishes and sauces are produced either by small cottage industries or, increasingly nowadays, by factories. Locally they are quite cheap, but as more and more are exported to the West these convenient relishes become pricey.

The recipes in this section are not too difficult or time-consuming to make; and in any case I give you the alternatives that you can buy in plastic containers or jars in many shops.

NAM JEEM

A sweet chilli sauce   Serves 6–8

Preparation time: 5 minutes + 10 minutes cooking

8–10 large red chillies, chopped

6 garlic cloves, chopped

125 ml (4 fl oz) water

½ teaspoon salt

2 teaspoons sugar

juice of 1 lemon

1 tablespoon fish sauce

1 tablespoon groundnut or olive oil

This chilli sauce can be used as a dip for Siu Mai (page 27), Tang Tong (page 30) or Koong Tord (page 46); or as an additional sauce to a rice dish. You only need a very small amount. This type of chilli sauce is available in bottles in Thai shops.

Put all the ingredients in a saucepan and bring them to the boil. Cover the saucepan and simmer for 10 minutes. Transfer everything to a blender or food processor, and blend until quite smooth. Adjust the seasoning, and transfer the sauce either to a small bowl, to be served straight away, or to a jar to be refrigerated until needed. It will keep in the fridge for up to 2 weeks.

NAM PRIK PAO

A hot chilli relish   Serves 6–8

Preparation and cooking time: 10 minutes

3 tablespoons groundnut or
olive oil

20 dried small red chillies,
soaked in water until soft
and drained

4 garlic cloves, chopped

5 shallots or 1 large onion,
chopped

6 tablespoons lemon juice

1 teaspoon sugar

1 tablespoon fish sauce

a large pinch of salt

*Like Nam Jeem (page 74) this relish can be used as a
dip, but it is also added to soup to make it really hot
and sour. It is much hotter than Nam Jeem because the
chillies used here are the very hot, small 'bird chillies',
either fresh or dried. I use the dried ones here, because
they are easier to get.*

Heat the oil in a wok or frying-pan, and fry the
chillies, garlic and shallots or onion, stirring all
the time, for 4 minutes. Cool. Then transfer the
whole lot, including the oil, to a blender or food
processor. Add the rest of the ingredients and
blend until smooth. Transfer the relish to a bowl
or a jar. Keep for a week in the fridge, or freeze.

SAMBAL TERONG

A hot aubergine relish   Serves 4–8

Preparation time: 20 minutes + 1 hour cooking

2 medium-size aubergines

2–3 tablespoons olive oil

1 onion, chopped finely

2 garlic cloves, chopped
finely

4 large green chillies, de-
seeded and chopped finely

1 teaspoon shrimp or
anchovy paste

1 teaspoon ground coriander

juice of 1 lemon

1 teaspoon sugar

1 teaspoon salt

2 tablespoons finely
chopped fresh mint

*This is a very good relish to eat with lamb dishes, such
as grilled lamb chops, lamb stew or roast lamb. It is
also good for canapés, on top of small pieces of toast.*

Preheat the oven to Gas Mark 4/180°C/350°F
and roast the aubergines whole for 35 minutes.
    When the aubergines are cool, cut them in half
lengthways, and scoop out the flesh with a
spoon. Put the flesh on a chopping board and
chop it finely.
    Heat the oil in a wok or frying-pan, and fry
the onion, garlic and chillies for 2 minutes,
stirring all the time. Add the rest of the
ingredients except the mint. Stir, and add the
mint. Adjust the seasoning and transfer to an
ovenproof dish. Cover the dish with foil, and
bake in the oven at Gas Mark 3/160°C/325°F for
25 minutes. Serve hot or cold.

SAMBAL KACANG

A peanut sauce   Makes about 300 ml (½ pint)

Preparation and cooking time: 25 minutes

125 ml (4 fl oz) groundnut
or sunflower oil

250 g (8 oz) raw peanuts

600 ml (1 pint) hot water

For the paste:

3 shallots or 1 onion,
chopped

3 garlic cloves, chopped

1 teaspoon shrimp paste
(optional)

½ teaspoon chilli powder

1 teaspoon ground coriander

½ teaspoon ground cumin

½ teaspoon sugar

1 tablespoon dark soy sauce

½ teaspoon salt

2 tablespoons tamarind
water (page 14) or lemon
juice

2 tablespoons olive oil

Here is a good satay sauce that you can make yourself without too much trouble. This is also the sauce used for Gado-Gado on page 72. The sauce is also known as Bumbu Saté or 'satay sauce'.

*Goreng Bawang
(Crispy fried shallots)*

Sambal Terong (A hot aubergine relish)

Heat the groundnut or sunflower oil in a wok or saucepan, and fry the peanuts for 4 minutes, stirring them frequently. Take them out with a slotted spoon and transfer them to a colander lined with absorbent paper. Leave them to cool, then grind them in a blender or coffee grinder to a fine powder.

Put all the ingredients for the paste in a blender or food processor and blend until smooth. Transfer this paste to a wok or a large shallow saucepan. Heat, and stir it frequently, for 3–4 minutes. Add the water and bring it to the boil. When it is boiling, add the ground peanuts, stir

Nam Prik Pao
(A hot chilli relish)

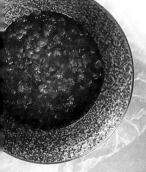

Sambal Kacang (A peanut sauce)

once or twice, cover the wok or pan, and simmer for 3 minutes. Uncover, and continue to simmer, stirring often, for another 2 minutes or until you get the thickness you prefer for your sauce. Adjust the seasoning.

You can keep this peanut sauce in a jar in the fridge until needed; it will keep for up to a week. It can also be frozen. Thaw it out completely before reheating it in a saucepan. You may need to add more water and continue heating it to get the right consistency.

GORENG BAWANG

Crispy fried shallots

Preparation and cooking time: 20 minutes

500 g (1 lb) shallots, sliced finely

150 ml (¼ pint) vegetable oil

Bawang *literally means onion, but in Indonesia and Malaysia our onions are shallots, or small red onions which are also the kind used in Thailand. In fact, the Thais use crispy fried garlic (available ready-made in Thai shops) more often than fried shallots. In Britain, crispy fried onions, made in Copenhagen, are available in supermarkets, and the ones made in Malaysia or Thailand are available in most oriental shops. If you want to make your own fried onions, use shallots, because they will become crisp without being coated with flour.*

Heat the oil in a wok or non-stick frying-pan until a slice of shallot dropped into it sizzles immediately. Fry the shallots in 2 batches, stirring all the time, for 3–4 minutes until they are crisp and golden-brown. Remove them with a slotted spoon and drain in a colander lined with absorbent paper. Leave them to cool before storing them in an airtight container. They will keep crisp in the container for about a week.

SAMBAL KELAPA

A hot coconut sambal   Serves 8–10

Preparation time: 6 minutes + 7–8 minutes cooking

2–3 tablespoons groundnut or olive oil

5 shallots or 1 large onion, chopped finely

2–4 garlic cloves, chopped finely

½–1 teaspoon chilli powder

1 teaspoon ground coriander

1 teaspoon fried shrimp paste, or anchovy paste

This is just a spicier version of the coconut dressing for Urap *(page 65). However, this recipe takes less time to prepare, because instead of freshly-grated coconut it uses desiccated coconut.*

Heat the oil in a wok or frying-pan, and fry the shallots or onion and the garlic for 2 minutes. Add the rest of the ingredients, except the coconut and lime or lemon juice. Stir the whole thing around and let it simmer for 1 minute. Then add the desiccated coconut and some salt.

300 ml (½ pint) water	Stir and simmer until all the water has been absorbed by the coconut. This will take 4–5 minutes. Add the lime or lemon juice and adjust the seasoning. Stir it around for a few more seconds. Transfer into a bowl, and serve hot or cold as a relish. This coconut sambal is particularly good with plain cooked brown rice.
½ teaspoon sugar (optional)	
125 g (4 oz) desiccated coconut	
juice of 1 lime or lemon	
salt to taste	

SAMBAL IKAN

A fish sambal   Serves 4–8

Preparation and cooking time: 25 minutes

198 g (7 oz) can of tuna fish, drained	*This recipe is taken from one of my other books,* Indonesian Food and Cookery, *(Prospect Books, 1986). This is the easiest way to make this sambal, which is a particularly good and versatile one – it can be used as a relish, or as a side dish with any kind of fried rice, or as a canapé, on top of slices of cucumber and small prawn crackers. You can make a double-quantity of this sauce, if convenient, and freeze it.*
175 ml (6 fl oz) coconut milk (page 10)	
For the paste:	
3 shallots, chopped	
4 garlic cloves, chopped	
4 candlenuts or 6 blanched almonds, chopped	Put all the ingredients for the paste into a blender or food processor, and blend until smooth. Transfer this paste to a wok or small saucepan, and heat it for 4 minutes, stirring most of the time. Add the tuna fish and the coconut milk, and stir and simmer until the mixture becomes thick. Adjust the seasoning and transfer to a bowl. This sambal can be served warm or cold.
3 small red chillies, or 1 teaspoon chilli powder	
2 tablespoons tamarind water (page 14) or 2 teaspoons tomato purée	
½ teaspoon brown sugar	
½ teaspoon salt	
2 tablespoons vegetable oil	

RICE AND NOODLES

Rice is the staple food of the three countries that I cover in this book, and we are very particular that the rice should be the best and should be cooked to perfection. If you have an electric rice steamer, then you are a big step ahead; your rice will come out perfect every time, unless you put too much water in.

Nasi Lemak (Coconut rice)

Nasi Kuning (Yellow savoury rice, page 87)

PLAIN COOKED RICE

Serves 4

2 cups long-grain rice, such
as basmati, Thai fragrant or
patna, or long-grain brown
rice

2 cups cold water

Lontong (Compressed rice)

*I shall not attempt to give you the Thai, Indonesian
and Malaysian names for this, as my other recipes for
savoury rice dishes are based on the plain cooked rice
described below. I must point out that the best way to
measure rice and the water to cook it in is to use the
same cup for both. For two cups of rice, you use two
cups of water. If you want your rice a little softer than
usual, you can add another ½ cup of water. But don't
add the extra water if you are going to use this rice to
make fried rice. And don't ever add salt to plain cooked
rice.*

Put the rice in a saucepan, and wash it in two
changes of water; pour in cold water till the rice
is well covered, swirl it around with your fingers
so that any impurities float to the surface, and
pour away as much water as you can without
losing the rice; then repeat the process. Add the
cold water, put the saucepan on a medium heat
and bring the rice to the boil. Stir with a wooden
spoon, and let this simmer, uncovered, until all
the water has been absorbed by the rice.

Four ways to finish cooking the rice:
1. The traditional Oriental way is to keep the
rice in the same saucepan and cover it tightly.
Lower the heat as much as possible, and leave the
rice undisturbed for 10–12 minutes.
Then put the saucepan on top of a wet
tea towel placed on your draining
board. After 3 minutes, uncover the
saucepan and transfer the rice to a
serving bowl. Serve it hot, or let it
cool if you are going to make
fried rice.
You will find that a layer of rice
about 5 mm

Plain Cooked Rice, dried and fried as a snack

(¼ inch) thick will come off the bottom of the saucepan, like a cake from a cake tin. In Indonesia, we call this rice-cake *intip*. Do not throw this away; dry it in the sun, or in the oven as if you were drying bread for breadcrumbs. When dry, break it into small pieces and store in an airtight container. When you have a good quantity, say 1 kg (2.2 lb) or so, deep-fry the pieces in hot oil until they are golden-brown. Sprinkle them with a little salt, and you have an unusual and delicious crisp snack to serve with drinks.

2. If you don't want to save this rice 'cake', transfer the rice from the pan to a steamer and steam for 10 minutes.

3. Another way to finish cooking the rice is to transfer it to an ovenproof dish. Cover the dish with buttered greaseproof paper, then with aluminium foil. Put it in a preheated oven at Gas Mark 4/180°C/350°F for 10–12 minutes.

4. Alternatively, transfer the rice to a suitable container which can be microwaved, cover it with microwave wrap, set the microwave oven to full power, and cook the rice for 4–5 minutes.

NASI LEMAK

Coconut rice   Serves 4–6

Preparation time: soaking + 20 minutes + 10–12 minutes cooking

2 cups Thai fragrant or basmati rice, soaked for 1 hour

2 tablespoons olive oil or clarified butter

2¼ cups coconut milk

1 teaspoon salt

1 pandanus leaf or bay leaf

If you think plain boiled rice is bland and uninteresting, try this coconut rice. This Malaysian Nasi Lemak is what Indonesians call nasi gurih *or* nasi uduk. *Like all the other rice dishes in this book, this really should be made with the best rice available, which means either Thai fragrant rice or basmati.*

Wash the rice and drain off the water. Heat the oil or butter in a saucepan, and stir-fry the rice for 3 minutes.

Add the coconut milk, salt and pandanus or bay leaf and boil until the rice has absorbed all the liquid. Lower the heat, put the lid on the saucepan as tightly as possible and leave to cook for 10–12 minutes. Alternatively, put the half-cooked rice into a rice steamer and steam for 10 minutes; or finish the cooking in a conventional or microwave oven, as described on page 82 for Plain Cooked Rice.

Discard the pandanus or bay leaf before serving. Serve hot.

LONTONG

Compressed rice   Serves 8–10

Preparation time: 15 minutes + 1¼ hours cooking

250 g (8 oz) long-grain, patna or Thai fragrant rice, washed and drained

2 bags, about 15 cm (6 inches) square, made from muslin or heatproof perforated paper

1.75 litres (3 pints) water (and more later)

a pinch of salt

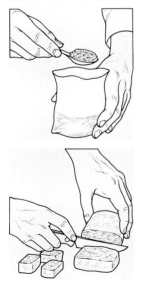

Compressed rice is always eaten cold, traditionally with satay, to soak up the hot satay sauce and give coolness against the hot sauce and a soft texture to contrast with the meat. In both Indonesia and Malaysia, the rice is cooked inside a roll of banana leaves. You can replace the banana leaves with aluminium foil, but much the easiest way of cooking Lontong is in a bag made of muslin (or heatproof perforated paper, if you can get it). Boil-in-the-bag rice ought to be ideal, and the bags indeed are excellent; unfortunately almost all such rice is now partially pre-cooked, and is hopeless for Lontong because the grains will not compress and merge together. If you can find boil-in-the-bag rice that is not pre-cooked, by all means use it. The cooking instructions are exactly as described below.

Fill the bags with the rice, making sure that each bag is only one-third full (1). Sew up the opening. Boil the water with the pinch of salt. When it is boiling, put in the bags of rice and let the water bubble gently for 1¼ hours. Add more water in the middle of cooking; the bags of rice must always be submerged. When cooking is finished, take out the bags – which should now be like plump, but rather hard, cushions – and drain in a colander. When they are cold, put them in the fridge until ready to use.

To serve, just discard the bags and cut the compressed rice into chunks with a large, sharp knife that has been wetted with water (2).

CHAR KWEE TAW

Singaporean rice-stick noodles with pork and prawns · Serves 4

Preparation time: 5 minutes + 15 minutes cooking

1.2 litres (2 pints) cold water

½ teaspoon salt

250 g (8 oz) rice-stick noodles

7 tablespoons groundnut oil

2 shallots or 1 small onion, sliced finely

2 tablespoons yellow bean sauce

a large pinch of chilli powder

125 g (4 oz) lean pork, sliced very thinly

125 g (4 oz) raw prawns, peeled and de-veined

3 shallots or 1 medium-size onion, sliced finely

3 garlic cloves, sliced finely

2.5 cm (1-inch) piece of fresh ginger, peeled and chopped finely

50 g (2 oz) bean sprouts

1 red pepper, de-seeded and cut into sticks

1 tablespoon light soy sauce

1 tablespoon dark soy sauce

3 tablespoons hot water or stock

4 spring onions, cut into 2 cm (¾-inch) lengths

salt and pepper to taste

Although these are called Singaporean rice-stick noodles, they are very popular all over Malaysia.

Put the cold water and salt in a saucepan, and bring it to the boil. When it is boiling add the rice-stick noodles, loosen and separate them with a large fork or wooden spoon and boil them for 2–3 minutes. Put them in a colander and rinse under a running cold tap until they are cold. Leave them in the colander to drain thoroughly.

Heat 2 tablespoons of the oil in a wok or large saucepan. Fry the shallots or onion for 1 minute, and add the yellow bean sauce and chilli powder. Stir for another minute, then add the noodles. Stir, turn and toss them until the noodles are hot. Transfer into a warm serving dish and keep this warm in the oven, covered with aluminium foil.

Wipe the wok or saucepan with kitchen paper, and add the other 5 tablespoons of oil. Heat and fry the slices of pork, stirring all the time, for 3 minutes. Take them out with a slotted spoon and drain them in a colander. Heat the oil again and fry the prawns for 2 minutes. Drain them on absorbent paper. In the same oil fry the shallots or onion, garlic and ginger for 1 minute, then add the bean sprouts, pepper, the two kinds of soy sauce, and the hot water or stock. Let this mixture simmer for 2 minutes. Turn up the heat and put the pork and prawns in, and add the rest of the ingredients. Stir everything around for another minute. Adjust the seasoning. Then pour the mixture over the noodles and serve hot.

Char Kwee Taw (Singaporean rice-stick noodles with pork and prawns)
Ba Mee Lahd Nah (Fried egg-noodles with chicken and bamboo shoots)

BA MEE LAHD NAH

Fried egg-noodles with chicken and bamboo shoots   Serves 4

Preparation and cooking time: 25 minutes

1.2 litres (2 pints) water

½ teaspoon salt, plus extra to taste

250 g (8 oz) fresh or dried egg-noodles

2–3 tablespoons groundnut or sunflower oil

4 shallots or one medium-size onion, sliced finely

2 garlic cloves, sliced finely

2.5 cm (1-inch) piece of fresh ginger, peeled and sliced finely

1 boneless, skinless chicken breast, sliced thinly

125 g (4 oz) can of bamboo shoots, drained, rinsed and sliced thinly

1 tablespoon fish sauce

2 tablespoons light soy sauce

¾ teaspoon ground white pepper

½ teaspoon sugar

4 tablespoons hot water or chicken stock

3 spring onions, sliced thinly

For these Thai fried noodles, I recommend using easily available dried Chinese egg-noodles, or fresh egg-noodles which are available in Chinese shops: I find other kinds of dried egg-noodles are a bit stodgy when cooked. I am told that the Chinese have a secret method of making their noodles so that they have just the right elasticity and are not brittle or stodgy. Noodles must never be overcooked.

Boil the water in a large saucepan with the ½ teaspoon of salt and add the noodles. If you are using fresh noodles, boil them for 1–1½ minutes; if using dried noodles, boil them for 3 minutes. Separate the noodles, using a large fork or a wooden spoon, while they are boiling. Put them in a colander under cold running water until they are cold, to stop them overcooking. Let the noodles drain in the colander, turning them several times so that all the water can drain off them.

Heat the oil in a wok or large shallow saucepan (preferably a non-stick one), and fry the shallots or onion, and garlic and ginger, for 1 minute. Add the chicken slices and bamboo shoots, stir-fry for another minute, then add the other ingredients *except* the noodles, hot water or stock, and spring onions. Keep stirring and turning the contents of the pan over for 3–4 minutes until the chicken is cooked. Add the hot water or stock, turn up the heat and add the noodles. Continue stirring, turning and tossing until the noodles are hot. Add the spring onions, and stir once more. Taste and adjust the seasoning. Transfer to a warm serving dish and serve immediately.

NASI KUNING

Yellow savoury rice   Serves 4–6

Preparation time: soaking + 5 minutes + 25 minutes cooking

500 g (1 lb) long-grain rice,
such as basmati, Thai
fragrant or patna

2 tablespoons vegetable oil

3 shallots or 1 small onion,
sliced finely

1 teaspoon ground turmeric

1 teaspoon ground coriander

½ teaspoon ground cumin

600 ml (1 pint) coconut
milk (page 10) or stock

1 cinnamon stick

2 cloves

½ teaspoon salt

1 kaffir lime or bay leaf

In Indonesia any thanksgiving party will have yellow rice at the centre of the feast, and in Bali yellow rice is also one of the important offerings to the gods in the temples.

Soak the rice for 1 hour, wash, and drain. Heat the oil in a saucepan and fry the sliced shallots or onion, stirring all the time, for 2 minutes. Add the rice, turmeric, coriander and cumin, stir-fry for another 2 minutes, and then put in the coconut milk or stock and the other ingredients. Boil the mixture, uncovered, stirring it once or twice with a wooden spoon, until the liquid has been soaked up by the rice. Then steam for 10 minutes. Alternatively, just cover the saucepan tightly and leave on a low heat, undisturbed, for 10 minutes; or finish cooking in the oven or microwave, as for Plain Cooked Rice (page 82). Transfer it to a serving dish, and take out and discard the cinnamon stick, cloves and kaffir lime or bay leaf. Serve hot as an accompaniment to savoury meat or fish dishes and vegetables.

NASI GORENG

Fried rice   Serves 4–6

Preparation time: 25 minutes + cooling + 10 minutes cooking

2 tablespoons vegetable oil

1 tablespoon butter

3 shallots or 1 small onion,
sliced finely

2 garlic cloves, sliced finely
(optional)

2 red chillies, de-seeded and
chopped finely, or ½
teaspoon chilli powder

This is only one of many variations of Nasi Goreng. This particular recipe is good for freezing. You can vary the trimming and garnishes to suit your taste; but even the most elaborate Nasi Goreng is quick to make.

Heat the oil and butter in a wok or large shallow saucepan. Fry the shallots or onion, garlic and chillies for a minute or so, then add the other ingredients except the rice, and stir-fry for 5 minutes or more until the vegetables are cooked.

	Then add the rice, and mix it well with the vegetables by stirring continuously until the rice is hot. Taste, and add salt or more soy sauce if necessary. Serve hot in a warm serving dish, garnished with sliced cucumber, tomatoes, and fried onion; or serve without the garnishes as an accompaniment to roast meat or other savoury main dishes. *Pictured on page 4.*

1 tablespoon light soy sauce

1 teaspoon paprika

2 teaspoons tomato purée or tomato ketchup

125 g (4 oz) button mushrooms, wiped and sliced

3 medium-size carrots, diced

2 cups of rice, cooked (page 81)

salt to taste

To garnish:

cucumber slices

tomato slices

fried onions

Then add the rice, and mix it well with the vegetables by stirring continuously until the rice is hot. Taste, and add salt or more soy sauce if necessary. Serve hot in a warm serving dish, garnished with sliced cucumber, tomatoes, and fried onion; or serve without the garnishes as an accompaniment to roast meat or other savoury main dishes. *Pictured on page 4.*

Note: This fried rice can be frozen for 1–2 months. Thaw completely before reheating in the oven at Gas Mark 4/180°C/350°F for 15–20 minutes. Cover the rice with aluminium foil to prevent drying. Alternatively, heat it in a microwave oven at full power for 4 minutes.

NASI KEBULI

Savoury rice with crispy fried chicken   Serves 4–6

Preparation time: 15 minutes + soaking + 1¼ hours cooking

2 cups (about 500 g or 1 lb) long-grain rice, such as basmati, Thai fragrant or patna

450 ml (¾ pint) vegetable oil

For the stock:

1.5–1.7 kg (3¼–4 lb) roasting chicken, cut into 8–10 pieces

4 shallots or 1 onion, chopped

3 garlic cloves, chopped

2 teaspoons ground coriander

1 teaspoon ground cumin

Nasi *is the Indonesian word for cooked rice. Nasi Kebuli is almost a meal in itself, and certainly needs no more than the addition of vegetables or salad.*

Soak the rice in cold water for 1 hour.

Meanwhile put the chicken and all the stock ingredients into a saucepan, and pour in the cold water. Boil the chicken until it is tender; this should take 30–45 minutes. Start on the next stage about 10 minutes before the chicken is ready.

Clean the rice by washing it several times in cold water; drain in a colander. Fry the rice for 5 minutes in a saucepan with 2 tablespoons of oil, stirring it all the time. Then strain off the stock from the chicken and add it to the rice. (You need a cup of stock for every cup of rice; if you find you have less stock than this, add water so

a pinch of ground galingale (optional)

5 cm (2-inch) piece of fresh lemon grass

a small cinnamon stick

a pinch of grated nutmeg

2 cloves

1½ teaspoons salt

1.5 litres (2½ pints) cold water

To garnish:

1 tablespoon Goreng Bawang (Crispy fried shallots, page 78)

a few leaves of fresh parsley

2 teaspoons chopped fresh chives

sliced cucumber

that you have enough.) Boil the rice in this stock until all the liquid has been absorbed – which takes only a few minutes. Then put the rice into a steamer and steam it for 10 minutes. Alternatively, proceed as for Plain Cooked Rice (page 82).

While the rice is cooking, deep-fry the chicken in the remaining oil. When everything is ready, serve on a large dish, with the rice piled up in the centre, the chicken portions arranged round it, and the pile of rice garnished with shallots, chives, parsley and cucumber. *Pictured on the front cover.*

GLUTINOUS RICE COOKED WITH COCONUT MILK

Serves 8–10

Preparation time: 10 minutes + 25 minutes cooking

500 g (1 lb) white glutinous rice

600 ml (1 pint) coconut milk, made from 175 g (6 oz) desiccated coconut (page 10)

a large pinch of salt

Glutinous rice or sticky rice is now easily available in Britain. In all the three countries covered in this book, sticky rice is used quite a lot, though not for everyday consumption. It is much richer and more filling than ordinary rice, so you only eat a small amount.

Wash the rice, and drain it. Then put it in a saucepan with the coconut milk and salt. Bring it to the boil and let it simmer, stirring it once or twice, until all the coconut milk has been absorbed. Then steam it for 15 minutes, or use the saucepan method (method 1, as described on page 82). For glutinous rice the two other methods – with a conventional oven or microwave – are not very satisfactory. Serve hot or cold, as for ordinary rice.

SWEETS AND DRINKS

The recipes in this section are for things that we usually eat, not as desserts, but as teatime snacks or between meals. In Indonesia and Malaysia, we eat these sweets to break our fast after sunset during Ramadhan, the Moslem fasting month, before we have our main meal. We don't, in fact, eat anything that corresponds to an English 'pudding' – we end a meal always with fresh fruit, and that is what I generally recommend people to do here as well.

BUBUR KETAN HITAM

Black rice porridge   Serves 4–6

Preparation time: soaking + 50–70 minutes cooking

75 g (3 oz) black glutinous rice, soaked for 2–8 hours, then drained, or 75 g (3 oz) pudding rice

1.75 litres (3 pints) coconut milk, made from 300 g (10 oz) desiccated coconut (page 10)

½ teaspoon salt

1 small stick of cinnamon

2 tablespoons brown sugar

I was quite surprised when several of my foodie friends asked me for this recipe, because I thought this kind of thing would not appeal to Westerners. But in fact it is a delicious porridge, with a lovely purple colour, the same colour as blackberry purée.

Black glutinous rice is available in most Chinese or Japanese grocery shops, and in health food shops. Short-grain pudding rice can be substituted: it doesn't have the same colour or flavour, but still tastes delicious. It will take the shorter time to cook and doesn't need soaking.

Reserve 250 ml (8 fl oz) of the coconut milk to be used later. Put the rest of the coconut milk in a saucepan with the rice, add the salt and cinnamon stick and bring to the boil. Simmer slowly for 10 minutes, then add the sugar. Continue to simmer, stirring it often, until the porridge is thick. The whole cooking time will be 50–70 minutes. Pour the porridge into a bowl, and discard the cinnamon stick. Serve warm or chilled, like rice pudding. Warm the reserved coconut milk with a large pinch of salt in a saucepan for a few seconds, and then serve with the rice. Alternatively, you can serve single cream. *Pictured on page 4.*

PISANG GORENG

Fried bananas   Serves 4–6

Preparation and cooking time: 30 minutes

100 g (3½ oz) rice flour or
plain flour

25 g (1 oz) butter, melted

125 ml (4 fl oz) coconut
milk, made from 3
tablespoons creamed coconut
and 125 ml (4 fl oz) hot
water

a pinch of salt

4 medium-size fairly ripe
bananas

clarified butter or 150 ml
(¼ pint) olive oil

icing sugar (optional)

In Indonesia and Malaysia we have several varieties
of banana that are especially good for cooking. This
recipe is good made with ordinary bananas, or with red
bananas or apple bananas if available.

Mix the flour, butter, coconut milk and salt into
a smooth batter, adding a little water, if
necessary, to get a coating consistency. Cut the
bananas into halves, then halve them again
lengthways. Coat well with batter and fry in
clarified butter or olive oil (3 or 4 pieces at a time)
for 2–3 minutes a side, until golden-brown.
They can be eaten hot or cold; sprinkle them
with some icing sugar if you wish. *Pictured on
page 5.*

MANGLAK

A coconut-milk drink with sweet basil seeds   Serves 6–8

Preparation time: 15 minutes

1 litre (1¾ pints) coconut
milk (page 10)

2 tablespoons caster sugar

a large pinch of salt

1 tablespoon basil seeds,
soaked in cold water for 10
minutes and strained

75 g–125 g (3–4 oz)
frozen or canned young
coconut flesh

If you like coconut-milk drinks, this one is unusually
good. Many oriental shops sell young coconut flesh in
cans or frozen. Strain the canned young coconut, and
throw away the water because it is far too sweet. If you
use frozen coconut, thaw it out completely before
adding it to the drink.

Warm the coconut milk with the sugar and salt,
until it is just at boiling point. Stir immediately
and take off the heat. Divide the soft basil seeds
and the young coconut among 6 or 8 glasses, and
pour the warm coconut milk in equal amounts
into the glasses. Leave for a while to infuse. If
you want this drink cold, put in some crushed
ice just before serving, but don't refrigerate it, as
the coconut milk will separate.

SEKOTENG

A hot gingery sherbet

Serves 6–8

Preparation and cooking time: 20 minutes

For the gingery drink:

1.2 litres (2 pints) water

10 cm (4-inch) piece of fresh
ginger, peeled and chopped

4 tablespoons granulated or
demerara sugar

For the titbits:

50 g (2 oz) peanuts

the seeds from one
pomegranate

2 slices of white bread,
cut into small cubes

2 tablespoons lemon
juice (optional)

In Java, the drink which is called sherbet anywhere else is called *wedang*, and a *wedang* is usually served hot or warm. Sekoteng is one of these. They are often sold in the street along with other street food. And all over Central Java sekoteng kits, or instant sekoteng, can be bought in shops and in the market, sold in little paper bags filled with titbits, usually coloured pink, and a sweet, gingery powder. You make it like making instant coffee; the whole contents

*Sekoteng (A hot
gingery sherbet)*

of the bag are put into a mug or a glass, and boiling water is poured over them. The Javanese will drink this at any time of day, instead of sweet tea or coffee. It is also an excellent drink for a cold winter evening, even though there are no such evenings in Java. Here is the recipe for one of the many variations of Sekoteng.

Put the water, ginger and sugar in a saucepan, bring to the boil, and simmer for 8–10 minutes, stirring occasionally to dissolve the sugar. At the same time, but in another saucepan, boil the peanuts for 10–12 minutes until soft, then drain them in a colander. Strain the sweet gingery liquid through a fine sieve into another saucepan. Bring it back to the boil, add the cooked peanuts, simmer for 2 minutes and add the rest of the ingredients. Take the saucepan off the heat, give it a stir, and serve the Sekoteng hot or warm in a glass, with a small long-handled spoon to eat the bits with.

Sankhaya (Coconut cream custard)

Mamuang Kuo Nieo (Mango with sweet glutinous rice)

SANKHAYA

| Coconut cream custard | Serves 4 |

Preparation time: 10 minutes + 20 minutes cooking

4 eggs (size 2)	*This is the Thai name for what in Indonesia is called serikaya. The Thais, and the Laotians, pour the Sankhaya into a seeded but whole pumpkin, steam the pumpkin, and serve it cold, cut into slices.*
6 tablespoons grated palm sugar or demerara sugar	
a pinch of salt	
175 ml (6 fl oz) very thick coconut milk (page 10)	Preheat the oven to Gas Mark 4/180°C/350°F. Beat the eggs lightly, add the sugar, salt and coconut milk, and stir until the sugar is dissolved. Divide this custard equally among 4 ramekins, and cook them in a bain-marie (which will give the best result) in the oven for 20–25 minutes. (They could also be steamed for 8–10 minutes.) Serve the Sankhaya cold with fresh fruit.
sliced peaches or nectarines, or strawberries, loganberries or raspberries, to serve	

MAMUANG KUO NIEO

| Mango with sweet glutinous rice | Serves 6–8 |

Preparation and cooking time: soaking + 30 minutes

2 cups glutinous rice	Soak the rice in cold water for 30 minutes.
600 ml (1 pint) coconut milk (page 10)	To cook the rice, drain it, and put it into a saucepan with the coconut milk, salt and sugar. Bring it to the boil and simmer, stirring it occasionally with a wooden spoon, until the rice has absorbed all the coconut milk and is very soft. Transfer the rice into a steamer or double saucepan and steam it for 15 minutes.
a pinch of salt	
2–3 tablespoons caster sugar	
4 small or 2 large mangoes, peeled and sliced or cubed	

Cool the rice a little. You can put the rice into individual moulds. It is advisable to line the moulds with cling film or foil, so that the rice can be unmoulded easily. To serve, turn out the moulds into the middle of the dessert plates, and arrange the cubes or slices of mango around.

Alternatively, spread the cooked glutinous rice on a tray lined with aluminium foil, then roll the rice flat with a wet rolling pin and cut it into diamond shapes with a sharp knife; serve as above.

INDEX TO RECIPES

Cover design: Barry Lowenhoff
Cover illustration: Sally Swabey
Text design: Ken Vail
Photography: Tim Imrie
Styling: Anna Tait
Food preparation for photography: Sri Owen
Illustration: John Woodcock
Typesetting: Hands Fotoset, Leicester
Origination: Colthouse Repro Ltd, Bournemouth